HOSEA

by

H. RONALD VANDERMEY

AMOS

by

GARY G. COHEN

MOODY PRESS
CHICAGO

All Scripture quotations, except those otherwise noted, are
from the *New American Standard Bible,* © 1960, 1962, 1963,
1968, 1971, 1972, 1973, 1975, and 1977 by The Lockman
Foundation and are used by permission.

Library of Congress Cataloging in Publication Data

Vandermey, H. Ronald.
   Hosea.
   Bibliography: pp. 79-80, 172.
   1. Bible. O.T. Hosea—Commentaries. 2. Bible. O.T.
Amos—Commentaries. I. Cohen, Gary G. Amos. 1981.
II. Title. III. Title: Amos.

BS1565.3.V34   224'.607   81-1781

ISBN 0-8024-2028-1   AACR2

2 3 4 5 6 7 Printing/LC/Year 87 86 85 84 83 82

Printed in the United States of America

CONTENTS

3

INTRODUCTION TO THE LATE EIGHTH-CENTURY PROPHETS

In the eighth century B.C. God sent "Four Prophetic Horsemen" to warn His sleeping people of the great dangers ahead. Those prophetic riders appeared out of nowhere, one by one, and shouted their sacred proclamations of the doom ahead. They warned the astonished crowds to flee to God for mercy and to abandon their sinful ways of living. The names of the four members of this noble band were Amos (764-755 B.C.), Hosea (755-717 B.C.), Isaiah (739-690 B.C.), and Micah (735-700 B.C.).[1] The exactness of dates for their years of prophesying is not certain in all cases. However, present biblical and extra-biblical data assure us that the dates are sufficiently accurate.

The excitement that surrounds the messages of these four men is the result mainly of their warnings' urgency. They lived during the final years of the Northern Kingdom (Israel) and were the spokesmen of God's final pleas to the wayward ten tribes of Israel. What an awesome responsibility was theirs—to deliver God's last warning to a heretofore blessed nation and to announce that, unless there was a national repentance soon, there would be a national doom shortly. These prophets addressed a nation living upon a shaky foundation, which supported tottering military and political beams. That situation—a sinful people living in days of luxury but political uncertainty—makes the messages of these men still relevant for today's man who lives well but yet is faced on every hand with threats of "wars and rumors of wars."

The beautiful thing is that the writings of these heralds of God, amid the proclamations of coming chastisement, also presented a solution to Israel's problem—national repentance and a return to God. These good physicians of the past still have within their biblical journals God's prescriptions for peace, both nationally and individually, if modern man will only take the

1. The dates above are taken from John C. Whitcomb, Jr.'s *Chart of the Old Testament Kings and Prophets* (Chicago: Moody, 1968).

prescriptions. Sadly, both Israel (the Northern Kingdom) and Judah (the Southern Kingdom) refused, and the prophesied miseries came upon them.

It is hoped that people today will learn some of the lessons from these ancient teachers and will experience the promised blessings, rather than the sure and certain punishments that are the portion of those who ignore God's teachings.

MICAH (735-700 B.C.)

Micah presented a message of woe not only to the ten northern tribes, but also to the Southern Kingdom of Judah, which was to fall a century and a quarter after the fall of her northern sister. As he stood safely in Jerusalem in 722 B.C., the prophet Micah heard tearfully that the unrepentant northern tribes were being destroyed and conquered by the cruel pagan giant Assyria. As he heard daily of towns and cities burning and of their people being captured and taken into captivity, he continued to rebuke the equally self-satisfied nation of Judah. As that news from the north drifted southward and stunned the minds of the people in Judah to the reality of God's prophetic dooms, Micah still rebuked them. Yet in the end Judah would not listen, and God would bring the fierce Babylonian hordes down upon her. The Babylonians came first in 605 B.C., then again in 597 B.C., and finally once more in 586 B.C. when even the Temple of Solomon was pulled down and burned. Oh, that our generation also would hear the call of Micah and be spared the agony of God's rod!

ISAIAH (739-690 B.C.)

Isaiah, like Micah, spoke from Jerusalem. Isaiah 28 denounces the sins of the Northern Kingdom, but almost all the rest of the book's sixty-six chapters warns and pleads with the Southern Kingdom to forsake her sins while there is yet time to repent. Yet his negative prophecies strike a positive note as they abound with the final solution to Israel's problems, the coming of the Messianic deliverer (Isa. 7:14; 9; 11; 52:13–53: 12).

AMOS (764-755 B.C.); HOSEA (755-717 B.C.)

Amos and Hosea, however, were the pair whom God used

(one right after the other, like their predecessors Elijah and
Elisha) to announce to both the Northern and Southern Kingdoms that His patience at last had ended and that their hour of
decision had arrived. They voiced the challenge that Israel and
Judah either must repent right then or face God's immediate
judgment of conquest and rapine by the merciless Assyrians. For
Israel, that would mean complete scattering of the population
within a generation and an end of the ten tribes as a nation. For
Judah, such judgment would mean the destruction of her land
by the rampaging Assyrians. It would also be a harbinger of
Judah's captivity at the hands of the Babylonians a century and
a half later. Thus, unrepentant sister followed unrepentant
sister in grief while God's prophets stood atop the hills, knocked
down the altars to Baal, and wept.

Amos especially portrays to us that in Samaria, the capital
city of Israel, kings and princes sat "at ease in Zion" (6:1),
trusting in their foreign policy to keep them safe, instead of
trusting in the Lord of Hosts. How much like that is modern
America, sitting rich and "at ease in Zion" as dishonesty, immorality, and unbelief threaten to engulf the character of a
once great nation. God is increasingly despised as profanity
and even blasphemies can be heard daily over TV—and few protest. We too, like Israel of the eighth century B.C., are wealthy,
strong, and trusting in our economy and foreign policy to deliver us, while Christ stands so often ignored as He knocks at
the door of the national heart and at the doors of individual
hearts (Rev. 3:20). Consider some of the major events of the
1970s; the similarity is so marked and plain that it is frighten-
ing—America's failure to reach its objectives in Vietnam, its
standing by while Cambodia was raped by the Khmer Rouge;
which was followed by the loss of the Panama Canal, the taking
of fifty American hostages in Iran, and then the Russian invasion of Afganistan. Surely those events have their roots in a
forsaking of God rather than merely in "foreign policy miscal-
culations."

Yet Hosea emphasizes that despite the severity of the coming
chastening, God's love will not entirely forsake those whom He
once loved. No, in the end times He will gather up Israel,
cleanse her, and restore her to a favor that will transcend even
His former first love for her. God's love and willingness to for-

give rings out to every generation that studies this prophet.
(Read 1 John 1:9 concerning confession and forgiveness.)

Both of these "prophets of doom" end their messages with
this assurance of God's abiding love for His ancient people and
His absolute pledge of their end-time cleansing and restoration
(Hos. 14; Amos 9:11-15).

Thus, like twin waterfalls, this pair of books pounds upon our
emotions and challenges our own spiritual lives. Judgment for
sin is guaranteed, but mercy is ready at the instant of true repentance. May these messages to God's historic people Israel
also challenge His people of today who, after seeing the calamities of our time—dishonesty, corruption, crime, profanity, persecution, war, starvation, immorality, and the specter of World
War III and nuclear disaster—too often fall asleep when instead
they should fall on their knees in prayer.

Woe to those who are at ease in Zion (Amos 6:1).

HOSEA

by

H. RONALD VANDERMEY

To my parents,
Dr. and Mrs. Robert B. Vandermey,
and to the congregation of the
Bethany Bible Presbyterian Church,
Glendale, California

1

INTRODUCTION TO HOSEA

THE SITUATION IN HOSEA'S DAY

When the prophetic mantle fell upon a youthful Israelite named Hosea ben Beeri, change was in the wind. Peace and prosperity, the twin blessings that had especially characterized Israel during the fifty years (800-750 B.C.) preceding Hosea's ministry, were slowly ebbing away. Drifting further and further from the course that the Almighty had charted for His people, the Israelites had deluded themselves into believing that they had escaped the curse of that ancient proverb: "Be sure your sin will find you out" (Num. 32:23). Instead, in the sight of a holy God they had made their own destruction more necessary than the annihilation of the heathen Canaanites six hundred years earlier (Deut. 7:1-5; Josh. 3:10; 7:1). Nevertheless, Israel was part of God's chosen people. In His mercy God sent to the nation one last prophet to sound the final warning blast to prevent her from plunging headlong into the abyss that had been created by her own sins.

The change that would sweep Israel into captivity had begun to manifest itself openly in the political sphere soon after the Word of the Lord first came to Hosea. The death of Israel's greatest monarch, Jeroboam II (793-753 B.C.), had brought an eclipse of Israel's glory and political stability. In effect, his death had brought an exchange of monarchy for anarchy. But that change had already made its presence fully known in the religious and social life of Israel, as can be seen by looking back into Israel's historical roots. Jeroboam I (931-910 B.C.) had planted the seeds of destruction when he led the ten northern tribes out of the hand of God's appointed ruling house (2 Sam. 7:13, 16). Having believed that the religion of the people was too tightly bound to Jerusalem, Jeroboam I, in an act of political expediency, set up golden calves at Dan and Bethel as images of Jehovah (1 Kings 12:25-33). When he had constituted idolatry as the official religion of Israel, Jeroboam I at the same time provided the first link in the chain of sin that had by Hosea's day completely enclosed the Northern Kingdom.

Baalism, the Canaanite religion that Elijah and Elisha would spend their careers routing (1 Kings 18—2 Kings 10), manifested itself openly thanks to Jeroboam's idols. By Hosea's day, Baalism had become an excuse for the ritualizing of sensuality. The people were taught that they were worshiping the same God that had brought them the abundance of the promised land. Jeroboam I was again responsible for that when he deceived the people with these words: "Behold your gods, O Israel, that brought you up from the land of Egypt" (1 Kings 12: 28). Through deception, one of Satan's prime tools, the people had confused the truth with lies. To tell the people of a nation, quite satisfied with the state of religion, that they were all wrong was the monumental task to which Hosea was commissioned.[1]

The decay of religion had meant a corresponding deterioration of the society's moral fiber. Detailed so thoroughly by Amos (Amos 5:10-17)—Hosea also witnessed what had been the total and unabashed compromise that reigned from the courtroom to the bedroom. Justice was determined by the highest bribe (Hos. 7:1-2; 10:13), whereas faithfulness in word and deed was extinct (11:12). Drunkenness (4:11) and open harlotry (4:14) had taken on epidemic proportions. Established by God as a testimony of His standards (Exod. 19:4-6), Israel had become like her wicked neighbors, blatantly disobeying the laws of God (Hos. 4:2-3).

Although the people had lived rather comfortably in their rebellion until Hosea's day, it was his task to tell them that the commandments that they had broken would now break them. Israel's political instability had come to resemble that of a modern Central American republic as a deadly game of monarchial

---

1. Baal (meaning "lord," "husband," or "owner") was the epithet of Hadad, the Canaanite god of the late autumn and winter rains upon which farmers were dependent. Using the analogy of Baal as a husband fertilizing the land (his wife), temple prostitution was carried on by the local shrines with the alleged hope that such acts would induce Baal to "have intercourse" with the earth. See James Luther Mays, *Hosea* (Philadelphia: Westminster, 1969), p. 25.

musical chairs kept the crown passing from the hand of one assassin to the next. Six months after his ascension to the throne, Zechariah, the son of Jeroboam II, was murdered by Shallum. Shallum's dynasty lasted but a month before he fell prey to an assassin, Menahem (752-742 B.C.). Menahem's ten-year reign witnessed a major complication of the situation: the awakening of Assyria through its able ruler Tiglath-pileser III (745-727 B.C.), who envisioned the occupation of Palestine as a gateway to Egypt and as an opening to commerce on the Mediterranean Sea. When the inevitable attack came, Menahem had realized the folly of resisting the enemy, and, by paying a tribute of one thousand talents of silver to Tiglath-pileser III (Pul in 2 Kings 15:19), had allowed his country to become a vassal state.

Menahem's handling of his external foe had served as the catalyst for the strengthening of a growing opposition movement within his own country. Pekah (752-732 B.C.), the leader of that rebellion, set up an opposition government, and he eventually seized the throne by assassinating Menahem's son and successor Pekahiah (742-740 B.C.). Vainly attempting to reconstruct the decaying nation, Pekah secured an alliance with Rezin, king of Syria. The political intrigues that resulted from this alliance caused the destruction of much of Israel in 734 B.C. and all of Syria in 732 B.C. (Isa. 7:1—8:18). Pekah was killed by Hoshea (732-722 B.C.), who ruled as a "puppet king" for Assyria over a much diminished kingdom—the hill country surrounding the city of Samaria. With the death of Tiglath—pileser III (727 B.C.), Hoshea rebelled against Assyria, thinking he could count on the help of Egypt (2 Kings 17:4). Unfortunately for Hoshea, Egypt was as inept as a "crushed reed" (2 Kings 18:21), and Hoshea fell into the hands of the Assyrians, who captured the city of Samaria (722 B.C.) after a three-year siege (2 Kings 17:5-6). According to Sargon II, the conquering king, 27,900 citizens of Samaria were deported to Upper Mesopotamia and Media.[2]

In such a day of adversity, one would expect the people to listen to the Word of the Lord. "Peace in our time" was no longer an alternative, the clouds of judgment would not blow away. Hosea cried that captivity was irreversibly imminent and

2. John Bright, *A History of Israel* (Philadelphia: Westminster, 1959), p. 258.

certain (Hos. 5:6-9; 9:7), yet the people refused to see the handwriting on the wall. Even when the enemy was besieging the walls of Samaria, the stony-hearted citizenry did not call upon the name of the Lord. They had forgotten God (4:1; 8:14).

HOSEA THE MAN

The name Hosea (*Hoshea* in Hebrew) means "salvation," and it is derived from the same Hebrew noun (*yesha*) that produced the names Joshua (Num. 13:8, 16) and Isaiah (Isa. 1:1). Ironically, Hoshea was also the name of Israel's last king.[3] If King Hoshea had hearkened to the Word of the Lord by the prophet Hosea, the land and her people would have been saved from God's judgment. Instead, the salvation that Hosea preached would have to be relegated to that great future day when righteousness shall rule (Hos. 14:4-7).

What kind of man was given the task of bringing the mixed tidings of judgment and salvation? Except for the text of the book of Hosea itself, the Old Testament is silent about the man Hosea. The lack of biographical data within the text forces us to hypothesize about the origin and occupation of this prophet of God. From the numerous geographical notations in the book (4:15; 5:1; 6:8; 9:15; 10:5, 8, 15; 12:11; 14:5-8), it has been assumed that Hosea was a native of the Northern Kingdom. The subject matter of Hosea's illustrations has prompted commentators to suggest that he was either a baker (7:4), a peasant farmer (8:7; 10:13), a priest (5:1), or a son of the prophets (1:2; 4:5; 9:7-8). To reconstruct the character of the prophet from the text would be impossible except that between the lines Hosea reveals his deep-seated love for his brethren. It is significant that rabbinic tradition, perhaps because it noted the unique involvement that Hosea had with his subject matter, classified Hosea as the greatest among his prophetic contemporaries.[4]

3. To keep the two names distinct, English translators have spelled the minor prophet's name without the second *h*. Three others in the Old Testament had the name *Hoshea:* Joshua (Num. 13:8); an Ephraimite chief (1 Chron. 27:20); and a chief under Nehemiah (Neh. 10:23).
4. Shalom Coleman, *Hosea Concepts in the Midrash and Talmud* (New York: Block, 1960), p. 43.

The primary stimulus for that involvement with his subject was Hosea's marriage to Gomer, detailed for us in chapters 1-3. Commanded by God to take a "wife of harlotry," Hosea married Gomer, the daughter of Diblaim, who bore him three children. Although Hosea knew of the wayward tendencies of Gomer when he took her to wife, his heart was broken as she deserted him for the sensual pleasures offered by that truly "adulterous generation." However, the worldly attractions for which Gomer clamored soon proved illusory, and she fell prey to some form of slavery. Throughout that period of estrangement, Hosea's love never faltered, and when the second command from God came he purchased her freedom and won her affection.[5]

Molded by this crucible of domestic tragedy, Hosea was particularly equipped to give his listeners a glimpse of the pain that God felt when Israel rejected His love and went "a whoring" after other gods. Israel was a harlot in every sphere of life: *religiously*, in seeking after other gods; *socially*, in creating a society of adulterers; and *politically*, in searching for the protection of foreign nations rather than Almighty God. Hosea's message was thus keynoted by a sense of urgency. So personally absorbed was Hosea with the message given him by God that he rarely prefaced his remarks with the familiar phrase "declares the LORD" (2:13, 16, 21; 11:11). The short, broken lines of discourse, the incompleted metaphors that appear and vanish on each page, and the seeming disregard for the fetters of regular grammar suggest the compulsion that Hosea felt. Faced with an adulterous wife and an adulterous nation, his terse words stain each page with the transgressions that he constantly observed being committed before his eyes. Do we grieve and object concerning the disregard that we observe in our society for the laws of God?

The message of Hosea is simple: the justice of God brings punishment for sin; the love of God brings restoration for repentance. After a personal illustration of God's sovereign plan of redemption in the life of the prophet (chaps. one-three), Hosea reveals God's holiness through an indictment of faithless Israel (chaps. four-seven), His justice through an announce-

5. For an excellent analysis of Hosea's marriage, check H. H. Rowley, "The Marriage of Hosea," *Bulletin of the John Rylands Library* 39, no. 1 (September 1956): 200-233.

ment of the penalty for that faithlessness (chaps. eight-ten), and His love through a proclamation of the certainty of the promise of national restoration (chaps. eleven-fourteen).

OUTLINE

I. Hosea's Marriage: A Revelation of the Heart of God
   (1:1—3:5)
   A. Harlot Wife and Faithful Husband (1:1—2:1)
      1. The commission from God (1:1-2)
      2. The bitter fruits of harlotry (1:3-9)
         a. Jezreel: God's judgment imminent (1:4-5)
         b. Lo-ruhamah: God's mercy withheld (1:6-7)
         c. Lo-ammi: God's love removed (1:8-9)
      3. The triumph of God's grace (1:10—2:1)
   B. The Perils of Profligacy and the Quest for Restoration
      (2:2-23)
      1. Israel indicted (2:2-5)
      2. Israel punished (2:6-13)
      3. Israel renewed and restored (2:14-23)
   C. Gomer's Redemption and Israel's Restoration (3:1-5)

II. Hosea's Message: Revealing the Character of God
    (4:1—14:9)
    A. God's Holiness Indicts an Unrepentant Israel
       (4:1—7:16)
       1. The subjects of indictment (4:1-19)
          a. The people indicted for breaking the command-
             ments (4:1-3)
          b. The leadership indicted for misleading the people
             (4:4-19)
       2. The inevitability of judgment (5:1-14)
          a. Inevitable because of Israel's harlotry (5:1-7)
          b. Inevitable because of God's holiness (5:8-14)
       3. The necessity of complete repentance (5:15—6:3)
       4. The impossibility of immediate restoration
          (6:4—7:16)
          a. Impossible because of Israel's lack of loyalty
             (6:4-11)
          b. Impossible because of Israel's secret sins (7:1-7)

2

GOD'S SOVEREIGNTY PRESERVES ISRAEL

I. Hosea's Marriage: A Revelation of the Heart of God (1:1–3:5)

A. HARLOT WIFE AND FAITHFUL HUSBAND (1:1–2:1)

1. *The commission from God* (1:1-2)

The perilous times in which Hosea received "the word of the LORD" are dated in the first verse of the book. Hosea prophesied between the reigns of the Judean kings Uzziah (767-739 B.C.) and Hezekiah (715-686 B.C.). Because, as suggested in the Introduction, Hosea was a native of the North, the priority that is given to the Judean kings over King Jeroboam II of Ephraim (Israel) demonstrates a recognition that God's promises are with the Davidic line and not with the usurpers who divided the kingdom (2 Sam. 7:8, 13, 16). As for the kings of his native land, Hosea lists only Jeroboam II, and a review of the lives of the six monarchs who followed confirms the opinion that in the North the monarchy died with Jeroboam II.

Because of the predictive nature of the text of Hosea, the recorded discourses occurred prior to the fall of Samaria (722 B.C.), although his personal ministry extended at least until the start of the reign of Hezekiah. The commencement of Hosea's ministry has been set at 755 B.C., which date would harmonize with the prediction of the end of the line of Jehu (753 B.C.) in "a little while" (1:4). Thus, Hosea's message would fall on the heels of the ministry of his predecessor Amos (764-755 B.C.). In his revelation of the unfathomable love of God, Hosea complements Amos's exposition of the law of God. Perhaps Hosea had had the opportunity to hear the unpopular prophet from Tekoa and to develop within himself the conviction that Israel must repent or perish. The lack of reticence to perform the command of the Lord showed that Hosea had caught a glimpse of the burden.

The difficulty of preaching to a nation derelict of duty was compounded by the personal nature of the first command to Hosea—to take a wife of harlotry and have children of harlotry. Perhaps writing at some subsequent point in his life, Hosea reviews his early ministry to show how God had providentially led him to Gomer, whose marital infidelity permitted him to sense some of the pain that the Almighty experienced through the harlotry of His bride, Israel. A particularly appropriate description of Israel's status before God, the motif of harlotry, is found throughout Hosea's writings (2:2-5; 3:3; 4:10-19; 5:3-4; 6:10; 9:1).

2. *The bitter fruits of harlotry* (1:3-9)

In a narrative that should be understood as an historical account, Hosea records the names of his wife and children and the symbolic warnings that were intended for the wayward nation. Fully aware of the kind of woman that God wanted him to marry, Hosea announces in verse 3 that he has married Gomer, the daughter of Diblaim. An explanation of the significance of her name is not included in the text. Knowing that the name *Gomer* comes from a verb root meaning "to end, to come to an end, to complete," Keil has suggested that the woman's name indicates that she would be brought to "completion" or "perfection" through her whoredom.[1] The obvious significance is that Gomer's faithlessness to her husband would parallel Israel's faithlessness to God.

Hosea's daughter and two sons are the bitter fruits of his adulterous wife. Labeled "children of harlotry" in verse 2, the designation need not imply that the children were not physically Hosea's, but rather that they shared the taint of their unfaithful mother's character. Accordingly, God wanted Israel to know that the judgment would fall not only upon the corporate nation (Gomer), but also on each individual who shared in the sin of the nation (the children of Gomer).

1. C. F. Keil and F. Delitzsch, *Commentary on the Old Testament in Ten Volumes,* trans. James Martin (Grand Rapids: Eerdmans, n.d.), 10:38.

a. Jezreel: God's judgment imminent (1:4-5). With the fourth verse, God begins to reveal His plan of retribution on His unrepentant people. The judgment for the accumulated sins of previous generations would now be meted out upon the generation to whom Hosea gave the final warning. Through desolation and captivity the Israelites would learn the meaning of Ezekiel's parable: "The fathers eat the sour grapes, but the children's teeth are set on edge" (Ezek. 18:2). Using the occasion of the birth of Hosea's children, God delivered a warning through the name attached to each child. Isaiah, a contemporary of Hosea, was also instructed by God to give his children names that would stand as symbols of future judgment (Isa. 8:3), and future redemption (Isa. 7:3).

The Lord commanded Hosea to name his first son *Jezreel,* which means in Hebrew "God scatters" or "God sows." The people of Hosea's day would have recognized this as the designation for the fruitful valley between the highlands of Samaria and Galilee. Because it lay in the midst of a rock strewn land, the Israelites said the valley was "sown by God," hence the name Jezreel.[2] But this fourth verse divulges another important reason for naming the boy Jezreel. It was in that historic valley that Jehu had displeased the Lord by committing an excessive bloodbath on the house of Ahab. Although he piously claimed that the slaughter was the Lord's will, Jehu's motives were inspired by political ambition rather than religious fervor (2 Kings 10:29, 31). God set a time clock of judgment that would last through four generations of the line of Jehu (2 Kings 10:30). The alarm would sound in "yet a little while," a prediction that came true with the assassination of Zechariah, the great grandson of Jehu (2 Kings 15:8-12).

Although Jezreel had been a sign of doom to the household of Jehu, it also bore a warning to the entire population. According to verse 5, the kingdom itself would be terminated in the Valley of Jezreel. Hosea lived to witness the fulfillment of that prophecy as the bow of Israel (a symbol of military strength)

2. The Valley of Jezreel is today the 10-mile-wide Plain of Esdraelon, extending from the Mediterranean Sea to the Jordan River. At the west edge of this valley lies Megiddo, the site of many historic battles as well as the final battle when all nations gather against Israel (Zech. 14:1-2; Rev. 16:16). See Frederick Tatford, *Prophet of a Broken Home* (Sussex: Prophetic Witness, 1974), p. 22.

was broken by the forces of *Shalmaneser* at Beth-arbel in the Jezreel plain (10:14; 2 Kings 17:5-6). The captivity that followed gave Jezreel a very bitter meaning for Israel, namely, the scattering throughout the world (2 Kings 17:18). At last Israel was awakened to the reality of God's justice, even though the consequences of spiritual adultery had been clear since the day Israel made the covenant with God in the desert (Lev. 26:33).

b. Lo-ruhamah: God's mercy withheld (1:6-7). As the birth-pangs for Gomer's second child intensified, the wrath of God for an unrepentant, stony-hearted people intensified. The Hebrew name *Lo-ruhamah*, translated "she has not obtained compassion," speaks of God's removal of the deepest form of compassion. Compassion, often used in Hebrew as the term for a mother's love for her child, had not been produced by the harlot Gomer.[3] Hosea could not even say that Gomer "bore him a son" (1:3), for the wayward character of his wife had begun to manifest itself. Just as Hosea's marital love and domestic peace had almost vanished through Gomer's profligacy, the Lord's compassion for His adulterous wife, Israel, had been stretched to the breaking point.

To intensify the warning to the Northern Kingdom, Hosea reveals that God's compassion had not departed from Judah. Whereas imminent doom awaited Israel, a miraculous deliverance would come to Judah. Indeed, when Judah in 701 B.C. faced the same Assyrian hordes that had destroyed Samaria, God had compassion on her and in one night caused 185,000 Assyrian soldiers to be slain by the Angel of the Lord (2 Kings 19:35; Isa. 37:36). But that would not be the only deliverance that would await Judah in the future, for this verse likewise points to the ultimate time "in the last day" when God will fight for His people (Zech. 14:3). From this prediction by Hosea Israel should have realized that God will have compassion on those who trust in Him and do not seek security through their own devices. (The people of Israel finally realized this fact, Hosea 14:3.)

c. Lo-ammi: God's love removed (1:8-9). The details in verse 8 underscore the historicity of this narrative in the life of

3. Gerhard Kittel, *Theological Dictionary of the New Testament*, trans. and ed. Geoffrey W. Bromiley (Grand Rapids: Eerdmans, 1964), 2:480-81.

the prophet. The weaning of Lo-ruhamah (weaning was a festival observed throughout the Orient) would have occurred when the child was two or three years old (cf. Gen. 21:8; 1 Sam. 1: 24).[4] Accordingly, the Israelites had been given two or three years to think about the warning of the withdrawal of God's compassion.

God's time clock for judgment had but one final alarm: *Lo-ammi. Jezreel* had promised a scattering of the people; *Lo-ruhamah*, the withdrawal of God's covenant mercy; and now *Lo-ammi*, the severing of Israel's peculiar position as God's covenant nation. Lo-ammi, meaning "not my people" in Hebrew, strikes at the very heart of the covenant of Sinai, in which God declared, "I will take you for My people, and I will be your God" (Exod. 6:7; see also Lev. 26:12; Deut. 26:17; 2 Sam. 7:24; Jer. 7:23). Strengthening the belief that verse 9 is a declaration of the severing of the Sinaitic Covenant is the fact that God directed Hosea to use the same word for "the LORD" that is used elsewhere *only* in Exodus 3:14 (where "I AM" is *ehyeh* in Hebrew), when the Lord revealed His covenant name. Hosea literally says: "I am not your I AM," a vow that should have struck terror in the heart of every Israelite. Had the Lord cut off Israel forever? The next three verses answer this question.

3. *The triumph of God's grace* (1:10—2:1)

Between verses 9 and 10 lie volumes of Jewish history that fulfill the judgment of Jezreel. To the anguished cry of the ages God will in that day answer: "I have surely heard Ephraim grieving, 'Thou hast chastised me . . . bring me back that I may be restored, for Thou art the LORD my God'" (Jer. 31:18). Through the inspiration of the Holy Spirit, Hosea is permitted to give his countrymen an outline of the events of that restoration, which he terms "the day of Jezreel." Six specific blessings may be seen in these three verses: national increase (v. 10*a*), spiritual awakening (v. 10*b*), national reunion (v. 11*a*), Messianic leadership (v. 11*b*), victory over foes (v. 11*c*), and a complete restoration of the covenant relationship (2:1).

The revelation of those future events must have staggered

4. James Freeman, *Manners and Customs in the Bible* (Plainfield, N.J.: Logos, 1972), p. 21.

the mind and heart of Hosea. The prophecy that the sons of Israel would be a numberless multitude, an allusion to the fulfillment of the Abrahamic Covenant (Gen. 22:17), must have been as bleak a hope to the generation that walked in chains to Assyria as it was to the generation that saw millions walk into the ovens of Germany. Remote also were the prospects of national salvation. For Hosea, who would certainly face discouragement as he preached to a generation deaf to the Word of God, the revelation that Israel would one day hear God say, "You are the sons of the living God," brought much comfort as he carried on his ministry.

In verse 11, the prophet centers his prophecy on the blessings of national reunion. In a day filled with civil wars, suspicions, and international intrigue (5:8-15; cf. Isa. 7:1—8:4), no one seemed interested in the reunion of the promised land. The blessings would fall on the people if they repented and reunited, but as it is today, men could not look beyond their own selfish interests. The change of heart that must come will be evident when Israel and Judah again look to *one leader* (Hebrew, *rosh echad*, a reference to the king in 1 Sam. 8:5). This appointment of one leader will come in the recognition of the Messiah, the One whom they (the Jews) have pierced (Jer. 23:5-6; Zech. 12:10). Although the promises of salvation and the visible return of the Messiah have been extended by God's grace to include the Gentiles (Rom. 2:10; 10:9-13; 11:11), the literal fulfillment for Judah and Israel has not been annulled (Rom. 11:26; Gal. 3:17).

Another event that will make the day of Jezreel great is that Israel "will go up from the land." Recalling in this phrase the departure of the twelve tribes of Israel out of Egypt (Exod. 14:30; cf. 2:14-15), Hosea discloses that a great exodus will take place again when the Jews return to their homeland out of the heathen world. Israel's return to the land will be marked by a reversal of the usual outcome of battles in the Valley of Jezreel. In that great day of Jezreel, Christ will rout the enemy out of the land and bring the nation the peace that has eluded it for the past four millennia. To that generation living when the Messiah returns, Jezreel will be the sign of God's sowing Israel into the promised land for all eternity (2:23; Ezek. 36:9-10).

According to verse 1 of the second chapter, the great day of

Jezreel occasions the reappearance of the names of Hosea's other children. Like Jezreel, they will one day be signs of blessing rather than judgment. That will be accomplished simply by dropping the Hebrew negative (*lo*), making the new names *Ammi*, "my people," and *Ruhamah*, "she has obtained compassion." That joyful scene prompts Hosea to call upon the Israelites to salute one another with their new names.

As the future restoration of Israel is previewed in these verses, one is brought to a deeper understanding of the sovereignty of God. The Lord will punish faithless Israel, and yet in the midst of that punishment, He will preserve His chosen people because of His eternal plan for them.

B. THE PERILS OF PROFLIGACY AND THE QUEST FOR RESTORATION (2:2-23)

Hosea's own personal tragedy recedes into the background as Israel herself is examined under God's searchlight. The reasons for judgment recorded in this chapter form the outline of the contents of the second section of the book, chapters 4-14.

1. *Israel indicted* (2:2-5)

Continuing the imagery of Israel as the harlot wife, the Lord in verse 2 calls upon the harlot's children to indict their mother because of her adultery. "Contend" denotes a legal action, and the picture of courtroom justice seen in verses 2-5 corresponds to Hosea's sermons in chapters 4-7, which deal with the indictment of Israel for her sin. Although the husband is prosecuting his wife in a legal fashion, restoration, *not divorce*, is the goal of this action. With a heart of sorrow God declares: "She is not my wife." Experientially, Israel had broken her "marriage covenant" with God. In addressing Himself to the children of the harlot, the Lord acknowledges that although the nation would be judged for idolatry, a remnant within the nation would be saved.[5] Seven hundred years later, the apostle Paul offered the same promise as he "contended" with the Israelites of his day (Rom. 11:1-5).

The motivation for the children of the harlot to plead with their mother is in the consequences that would occur if the mother failed to give up the vestiges of harlotry (2:3-5). Again,

5. Keil and Delitzsch, 10:51.

the threat has the goal of restoration, for the Lord in His gracious covenant-keeping love vows to punish Israel with the lesser punishment for adultery. Rather than death by fire or stoning (see Gen. 38:24; Lev. 20:10; 21:9; Deut. 22:23-24), the Lord states that He will "strip her naked and expose her as on the day when she was born" (cf. Ezek. 16:39; Nah. 3:5). In giving this lesser punishment, the Lord takes the opportunity to remind Israel of her humble birth and early dependence upon God in the wilderness. Because Israel now credits Baal for the abundance in the land, God warns His people that they will again be cast into a desert land (v. 3).

Just in case the individuals to whom these words were addressed, "the children of harlotry," thought they would escape the punishment for the corporate nation, the Lord straightened them out (v. 4). Because they were children of harlotry, the corrupt tendencies of the nation had infected every individual to the extent that each one had endorsed and enjoyed the sinful practices of his mother. Hosea's generation was deaf to the pleadings of Jehovah. Through years of degeneration, the people had trained themselves to respond only on a physical level. A sensual religion devoid of spirituality was all they could understand. Truly, there was no knowledge of God in the land (4:1).

Once the children have been notified of their inclusion in this indictment, the Lord as plaintiff concludes his indictment in verse 5 by revealing the heinousness of the crime. In summing up his case, the plaintiff quotes these shameful words from his unloving wife: "I will go after my lovers, who give me my bread and my water, my wool and my flax, my oil and my drink." Hebrew grammar denotes Israel's statement "I will go" as a designation for intense, passionate love, and it can be translated "let me go." Israel, willing to believe a lie, credits her false lovers (Baal) for every good thing she has received: bread and water (the necessities of life); wool and flax (the necessities of warm and cool weather); oil and drink (health and luxury items).

2. *Israel punished* (2:6-13)

The punishment promised for the indicted nation, detailed in chapters 8-10, is now outlined in verses 6-13 of chapter 2. The section is introduced by "therefore," a word used frequently in Hebrew prophecy as an announcement of some action that the Lord is about to take in response to the sufferings or deeds of His people.[6] Hosea uses "therefore" three times to introduce judgment upon Israel (2:6, 9; 13:3), and once to introduce God's plan for the restoration of Israel (2:14).

Verses 6-8 summarize God's initiation of the process of punishment, the isolation of Israel from her illicit lovers. As was seen previously in the indictment, God's actions have in view the restoration of Israel. God chooses not to slay His harlot wife, but rather to build a hedge around her. Job employs the term "hedge up" to refer to God's providential care for His people (Job 1:10; 10:11-12), and this same providential care is in evidence in Hosea as God chooses to remove all temptations from His wife. Likening His adulterous wife to a vineyard, God builds around her both a hedge and a wall (protective parts of a vineyard). Israel, rebellious to God's strategy for rehabilitation, begins a "vehement pursuit" and a "diligent search" (intensive Hebrew verbs) for the elusive Baalism (v. 7). This search for a renewal of the so-called blessings from idols will end in frustration. Then Israel will return to her first husband, having remembered that she was blessed only when she was in a right relationship with God. According to Hebrews 12, believers today also can expect the discipline of the Lord when they stray from His will.

The root cause of Israel's waywardness may be traced to one thing: her lack of *knowledge*. God had given her sufficient knowledge of the source of her blessings as well as knowledge of the punishment that would come for ignoring that source. In Deuteronomy, God specifically states that it is He who will give them the grain, the wine, and the oil (Deut. 7:13; 11:14), and that it is He who will remove this trio of blessings if the people rebel (Deut. 28:51). According to Hosea 2:8, Israel did not know God. In the metaphor of a husband and wife, the word *know* (*yada'* in Hebrew) speaks of the oneness that exists between a husband and his wife (Gen. 4:1).[7]

6. Hans Walter Wolff, *Hosea,* trans. Gary Stansell, ed. Paul D. Hanson (Philadelphia: Fortress, 1974), p. 35.
7. As one of the major themes of his sermons to wayward Israel, Hosea develops the concept of knowledge in 2:20; 4:1-6; 5:3-4; 6:3-6; 7:9; 8:2; and 9:7.

The grave consequences of forgetting the Lord, detailed in verses 9-13, emphasize the Lord's desire for Israel to know Him again. Thirteen times in these five verses the Lord speaks of Himself by the first person personal pronoun, which accentuates that it was *He* who was taking away the blessings that *He* had bestowed upon Israel. The failure of the harvest (the first stroke of judgment) left Israel naked before "her lovers." From the decay that had occurred in the religious, social, and political scene in Israel, the false lovers should include not only the false gods, but also the social immorality that characterized their lives, and the political immorality of attempting to find security in foreign alliances. An end to the harvest meant an end to all the festivals that Israel had enjoyed, a fitting punishment because Jeroboam I had altered the divinely appointed setting for those feasts (1 Kings 12:32).

The predicted destruction of the vine and fig tree in verse 12 should have shaken Israel to an awareness of her folly. The vine and fig tree were not simply agricultural products, they were symbols of the sustenance of life, which included peace and prosperity in the Palestinian homeland (Mic. 4:4; Zech. 3:10). Although these symbols are again popular in the state of Israel today, the Israelites of Hosea's day would forfeit these symbols because they had considered them to be the wages given to them by their false lovers.

Verse 13 issues the last prediction of punishment, made necessary because Israel had been "faithful" in her observance of the "days of the Baals."[8] The same people who forgot the Lord who brought them out of the house of bondage never forgot to adorn themselves properly for a festival dedicated to Baal. Unfortunately, many today who consider themselves to be Christians forget the Lord on His day, but they religiously remember to watch the Sunday ball game on television or play that early morning round of golf.

3. *Israel renewed and restored* (2:14-23)

In the same way as he later concludes his prophecy with a message of hope for the children of Israel (chaps. 11-14), Hosea

8. Baal (see page 12, fn. 1) had become a collective term for the Canaanite gods including Baal-berith, "the lord of covenants" (Judg. 8:33); and Baal-zebub, "lord of the flies" (2 Kings 1:2). Baals were also associated with various towns (Josh. 11:17; 2 Kings 4:42).

now employs the remaining verses of this chapter in a description of the renewal and restoration that God will effect for Israel. Both the sovereignty and the grace of God are beautifully blended in the first words of verse 14: "Therefore, behold, I will allure her." Although He has spoken harshly to Israel from His throne of judgment, the Lord now will "speak kindly to her" (literally, "speaks to her heart"; cf. Gen. 50:21). Credit for this change in the position of the harlot wife belongs to the corrective force of Israel's punishment, which has stripped away all the tantalizing allurements of the world and placed Israel in a position of isolation where she can hear only God's voice. It is fitting that the place for that change to occur is the wilderness, where God first spoke to Israel (cf. Ezek. 20:33-38).

Having the features of a "second honeymoon," the scene in the fifteenth verse pictures a reenactment of that first entrance into the promised land. The Lord gives Israel "her vineyards [symbolic of renewed peace and prosperity] from there," that is, from the east coming over the Jordan River. With Israel's sin fully judged in advance, the Valley of Achor, the site of troubling for Israel when she first entered the land (Josh. 7), would now be a "door of hope" (see also Isa. 65:10). The joyousness of this return to the land will provoke Israel to sing the Song of Moses once again, as she did when the Lord brought her through the Red Sea (Exod. 15:1-21). It is interesting to note that the Song of Moses also will be sung in the Tribulation by those who overcome the Beast (Rev. 15:2-3).

Verse 16 is significant for its introduction of the words "in that day," one of the Old Testament technical terms for the *day of the Lord*, in which Israel suffers the Tribulation, the Messiah returns to defeat the enemies of Jerusalem, and the Millennial Kingdom is established (see Zech. 14:4-21). Because all Israel will be saved at that time (Rom. 11:25-26), the Lord declares that Israel will call Him *Ishi* ("my husband") rather than *Baali* ("my master, my owner, my lord"). This declaration by the Lord will mean an end to the deadly syncretism by which Israel had combined the biblical regulations for worship with the heathen Canaanite practices.

With Baal no longer the master of Israel, the Lord vows in verse 17 that Israel will completely forget her fall into idolatry. As if they were undesirable words on a blackboard slate, the

Lord will erase the names of the Baals from the minds and hearts of His chosen people.

The ramifications of the reconciliation between Israel and God extend to the natural environment, as Hosea records in verses 18-23. The animal kingdom, which has been hostile to man since the Fall, will have a covenant made between mankind and itself.[9] The animal kingdom, which will have been used by God to judge Israel for her wickedness (2:12), will now be a source of blessing to the reconstituted nation.

Along with the peace made with the natural environment, Israel will finally experience the establishment of a lasting peace with her neighbors. Just as the nature of all beasts has to be changed, so also the hearts of all mankind must be changed by the Lord before Israel can at last sleep in peace (Isa. 14:30; Jer. 23:6; Ezek. 34:25; Mic. 5:3; Zech. 14:11). Until the Prince of Peace conquers a world in rebellion to His authority, even the most valiant human endeavors to bring a "just and lasting peace" to the Middle East will be foiled (cf. Jer. 6:4; 8:11, 15; Ezek. 13:10, 16; Dan. 8:25).

Directing His attention once again to His bride, the Lord in verses 19-20 removes the separation that had been caused by Israel's adultery. In an act of gracious forgiveness, the Lord betroths Himself to Israel once again. By employing the term *betroth* (Hebrew, *aras;* literally, "to woo a virgin"), God reveals to Israel that He has not only forgiven the past, He has forgotten it also. The indissolubility of this marriage bond is guaranteed by each of these divine characteristics: His eternality ("forever"); His imputed righteousness ("in righteousness and in justice"); His covenant-keeping love (*chesed,* "lovingkindness"); His tender mercy (*ruhamah,* "compassion"); and His unquestionable "faithfulness." When the people of Israel have received the full impact of God's dealings with them, they will "know the Lord." The Lord Jesus Christ prayed in the garden to His Father, "And this is eternal life, that they may know

9. The making of a covenant with the animal kingdom is a picturesque expression, since in Hebrew the words *karath berith* mean literally "to cut a covenant," a reference to the custom of cutting an animal in two pieces. Both parties making the covenant would pass between the pieces of the animal. They would recite the terms of the covenant and the judgments that would befall the one who broke the covenant.

Thee, the only true God, and Jesus Christ whom Thou hast sent"
(John 17:3). Truly, this ability to know God, for us as well as
for Israel, is a gift of God, who loved us without our first having
loved Him (1 John 4:10).

Much like General Douglas MacArthur's famous promise "I
shall return!", the Lord emphatically declares in the closing
paragraph of the second chapter, "I will respond" (2:21). When
Israel knows the Lord in the fullest sense of *know*, then the Lord
will respond with all the blessings that had been promised so
long ago to Abraham (see Gen. 12:1-3; 17:2-16). God's response here means that the cycle of life is set into motion once
again. The divine response to the heavens produces rain upon
the earth; the response to the fertilized earth produces the staple
products necessary for sustaining life (Deut. 11:14); and those
staple products—the grain, the new wine, and the oil—in turn
respond to *Jezreel*, the people whom God has sown into the
land forever. The bitter fruits of harlotry—*Jezreel, Lo-ruhamah*,
and *Lo-ammi*—have been cast away as God announces in verse
23 that Israel will be sown in the land, that she will receive the
compassion of the Lord, and that the nation again will be the
people of the Lord. In reply to the renewal of these blessings,
Israel gives the answer that the Lord had desired for so many
years: "Thou art my God" (*Elohai* in the Hebrew).

C. GOMER'S REDEMPTION AND ISRAEL'S RESTORATION (3:1-5)

In the third chapter, the Lord makes known His plans for the
redemption of the prodigal nation. Although this chapter is
short, its prophecies survey God's past (v. 1), present (vv. 2-4),
and future (v. 5) relationships with Israel. Just as the prophet
Hosea had been commissioned to share, with God, the pain of
betrayal by a faithless bride, he is now commissioned to participate with God in the experience of bringing redemption to that
faithless bride.

The Lord's command in verse 1, "Go again, love a woman
who is loved by her husband," has stymied some interpreters
who wonder if the Lord is commanding Hosea to marry a
woman other than Gomer. Although their contention is based
primarily on the absence of Gomer's name in the third chapter,
the word *again* makes clear that Hosea is to love the one whom
he had previously loved. The analogy of the Lord's restoration

of His faithless bride, Israel, would be lost if the woman Hosea redeemed was not Gomer.

Hosea's unquenchable love for Gomer is modeled after the love that the Lord bestowed upon Israel. Like the woman Gomer, Israel had not returned that love, but had instead devoted herself to other gods and to "raisin cakes." Raisin cakes, sweetmeats made of pressed grapes, were symbolic of Israel's rebellion against the simplicity of her faith. Raisin cakes were an integral part of the ceremony in many Canaanite cultic festivals, including the ritual that honored the "queen of heaven" (Jer. 7:18; 44:19). Truly, the exchange of God's way for the allurements of pagan customs grieved the heart of the Almighty in Hosea's day, just as it did when the church of the Middle Ages submerged the truth of the gospel under a multitude of pagan doctrines. (Especially note the similarity of the cult of Mary to the ancient "queen of heaven" concept.)

Love is certainly the keynote of chapter 3. (The word *love* is repeated four times in the first verse.) Hosea's love for his wife causes him to be eager to redeem her, purify her, and take her back into his home and heart. Even though Hosea could have justified divorcing Gomer (Deut. 24:1), the command of the Lord to Hosea revealed to the prophet that grace was greater than the law. It is no wonder that many call this book "The Gospel According to Hosea."

The destitute state in which Hosea found his wife allowed him to purchase her for half the price of a common slave (Exod. 21:32). In addition to the fifteen shekels, Hosea gave fifteen ephahs of barley, the food of beasts. That action suggests that Gomer had degraded herself beneath human dignity. Although the redemption itself is accomplished in the second verse, the command of the Lord includes an indefinite period of testing before the husband and wife would be united in the full blessings of marriage. The verb *stay* (Hebrew, *yashab*) in verse 3 denotes an attitude of waiting in patient expectation (Deut. 21:13). With Gomer isolated from all temptations to revert to a life of harlotry, Hosea was permitted to devote all his efforts to wooing back his bride (2:14). The results of his efforts are not stated, but one can confidently speculate that at the end of that period of isolation Gomer responded to her husband's love. For the prophet, who had suffered the double heartbreak of a wayward wife and a wayward nation, the response of Gomer to his love gave him an experiential foretaste of that great day when Israel "will come trembling to the Lord" (v. 5) and say, "Thou art my God!" (2:23).

Just as Gomer would have to pass through a period of isolation, so also Israel is promised in verse 4 that she will be in isolation for "many days," during which time she would lose her desire for other gods. This undetermined length of time was especially needful because Israel had so completely confused the worship of the Lord with the worship of Baal. Accordingly, Israel would have to do without three vital elements during this period: political authority, ecclesiastical privilege, and prophetic revelation.

In Hosea's day, political authority was vested in a monarchy established by men in rebellion against God's appointed ruler (1 Kings 12:19-25). A major theme of the book of Hosea is the announcement of the downfall of this surrogate political system (5:1; 8:4, 10; 10:15; 13:10). Israel will also have to do without a prince (Hebrew, *sar* [5:10; 7:16]), the designation that is most likely a reference to the officers of the kingdom whose duties were in the military service of the land.[10] From the day of Hosea until our own day Israel has indeed remained without a king, and she will remain so until that great day when she acknowledges the Lord Jesus Christ as her King and Lord.

Regarding the ecclesiastical privilege that Israel had been granted, the Lord vows that they will be "without sacrifice or sacred pillar." The sacrifice, instituted by God as a foreshadow of the blood atonement of Christ, had been corrupted by the Israelites when they made the sacrifice at improper locations (Dan and Bethel; cf. 1 Cor. 12:29), with an improper priesthood (not the Aaronic line [Exod. 28:1]), and an improper motive (6:6; 8:11, 13). But the Israelites not only had abused the institutions that God had established, they also had worshiped that which was forbidden by God, including the "sacred pillar" (Hebrew, *matsebah* [Exod. 23:24; Deut. 16:22]).

Last of all, Israel would be "without ephod or household idols," the means by which she discerned the future. The ephod was a part of the garment worn by the high priest when he inquired of the Lord (Exod. 28:4). Whereas the ephod was a

10. James Luther Mays, *Hosea* (Philadelphia: Westminster, 1969), p. 58.

proper means of asking about the future, the household idols
(Hebrew, *teraphim*) were a means of divination of an entirely
pagan origin (see Ezek. 21:21; Zech. 10:2). As was the case
with their ecclesiastical privileges, Israel had ignored the divinely appointed means of divination and had sought out that
which was forbidden by God.

As with the end of chapters 1 and 2, in 3:5 the prophet looks
to the day when God will fulfill His purposes for His chosen
people. After "many days" of isolation, Israel will again seek
the Lord. When the Lord has wrought in their hearts this new
desire to seek Him, the ten tribes will finally realize that a return
to the Lord will mean a return to rulership by the house of
David, because the Lord promised the kingship to David's seed
forever (2 Sam. 7:13, 16). Both Christian and Jewish expositors
understand this to be a reference to the Messiah.[11] The time
designations "afterward" and "in the last days" speak of that
great Messianic era longed for by the children of Israel in all
ages.

When the people of Israel do return to the Lord "they will
come trembling" because of the afflictions that have brought
them to a place of utter helplessness (see also 5:15; 11:11; Mic.
7:17).[12] The many centuries of suffering experienced by the
people of Israel throughout the world will be culminated in the
Great Tribulation, the event that will bring the Lord out of
heaven to save His people Israel (see Zech. 14; Rev. 6-19).
Israel's return to God in the last days will truly be a return to
His goodness (Hebrew, *tobo*), that special place of blessing
where they will join in all the privileges of Christ's millennial
reign (see Isa. 52:7; Jer. 33:9; Zech. 9:17).

11. Shalom Coleman, *Hosea Concepts in the Midrash and Talmud* (New
     York: Block, 1960), p. 162.
12. Keil and Delitzsch, 10:73.

3

GOD'S HOLINESS INDICTS ISRAEL

II. HOSEA'S MESSAGE: REVEALING THE CHARACTER OF GOD
(4:1–14:9)

The sermons of Hosea, recorded in chapters 4-14, reveal three prominent characteristics of the God of Israel: His holiness (chaps. 4-7); His justice (chaps. 8-10); and His love (chaps. 11-14). Although each of these characteristics can be discerned in the analogy of the faithless wife and her faithful husband (chaps. 1-3), they are now disclosed in a manner whose depth is unparalleled in the rest of the Old Testament. As God's *holiness* demands that the nation of Israel receive an *indictment* for her sin, so also His *justice* requires that Israel should be *punished.* But in the midst of these two great attributes a third is at work: the *love* of God, which has as its chief goal the *restoration* of God's people to Himself.

A. GOD'S HOLINESS INDICTS AN UNREPENTANT ISRAEL (4:1–7:16)

Over seven hundred years after Hosea uttered his prophecy, the apostle John wrote, "The one who does not love does not know God, for God is love" (1 John 4:8). In Hosea's day the people of Israel had mistakenly assumed that God's love could be manifested to them without their knowing God. God through the prophet Hosea corrects that situation by first of all disclosing that He is a Holy God (see also Isa. 6:3). The illumination that Israel receives in Hosea 4-7 acts also as an indictment upon the kind of life the people had established in the darkness created by their own ignorance (4:6; cf. Eccles. 2:13-14; John 3:19; Rom. 13:12; 2 Cor. 4:6).

1. *The subjects of indictment* (4:1-19)

In order to get the attention of the whole house of Israel, the

Lord first commissioned the prophet to announce who it is who is to receive the indictment.

a. The people indicted for breaking the commandments (4: 1-3). Amid the deafening tumult of wickedness, Hosea steps before the nation with a subpoena from God (v. 1). The people who had ignored the Word of the Lord for the past two hundred years would at last be forced to listen to the charge that they had broken the covenant established at Sinai (Exod. 19:5; 34:27; Deut. 4:23; 31:16-17; cf. Mic. 6:2). This case against the inhabitants of the land finds the Holy One of Israel acting not only as the prosecuting attorney, but also as the plaintiff, the witness, the judge, and the executioner (cf. Amos 9:8).[1] With an indictment that includes both *sins of omission* (v. 1b) and *sins of commission* (v. 2), Israel would learn that nothing had escaped the watchful eye of the Lord (cf. Jer. 5:3; Ezek. 10:12; Amos 9:8).

In terms of that which had been omitted, the prophet laments that Israel had not cultivated within herself the three blessings that spoke of her unique covenant relationship to the Lord: *faithfulness, kindness,* and *the knowledge of God.* Faithfulness, which comes from a root word that means "to confirm, to sustain, to support" (Hebrew, *emeth;* literally, "truth"), was nowhere to be found because the people of Israel had not sustained or supported the covenant with God—a pattern that spilled over into their relationships with their fellow men (7:1, 2, 11; 10:13; 11:12). Kindness (Hebrew, *chesed;* often translated "lovingkindness, mercy, kindness, and loyalty") is that special Hebrew term for God's covenant love, which was first manifested to Israel in her redemption from Egypt (Exod. 15: 13). This covenant love will again be operative when God draws the whole house of Israel back to Himself (2:19; 10:12; 12:6; Jer. 31:1-3; cf. Psalms 17:7; 25:6; 69:16; 103:4; Isa. 63:7; Jer. 9:24; 16:5; 32:18).

Israel's inability to respond to God in faithfulness and kindness stemmed from her obstinate refusal to accept the knowledge (Hebrew, *da 'ath*) of God that had been imparted to her in the covenant (Exod. 3:15; 20:2-17). Because the land had been granted to Israel as the place where she might live by

1. Theodore Laetsch, *The Minor Prophets* (St. Louis: Concordia, 1956), p. 41.

those covenant obligations, the decision to live as rebels made the people, in effect, "squatters" who deserved eviction.

The natural consequence of that rebellion against the covenant of God is the scene described in the second verse. Israel is charged with breaking the commandments of God. Five of these are listed in rapid succession: swearing (see also 10:4; Exod. 20:7); deception (see also 7:13; 10:13; 12:1; Exod. 20:16); murder (see also 6:9; 9:13; Exod. 20:13); stealing (see also Exod. 20:15); and adultery (see also 4:14; Exod. 20:14).[2] Israel, in quenching the knowledge of God, had truly become a violent society. One cannot help but wonder if rulings such as the 1963 United States Supreme Court ban on prayer and Bible reading in the public schools have not contributed to the growth of America's permissive and violent society, which experiences almost a daily multiplication of crime in the streets. Reading the headlines of today's newspapers should prompt us to cry with Hosea, "Bloodshed follows bloodshed" (v. 2b). How long can such a society linger on the face of the earth? Hosea warns in verse 3 that the moral decay had covered the entire land with a pollution that would sweep away all life (cf. Isa. 24:4-7; 33:8-9; Jer. 12:4, 11; Joel 1:10). Indeed, the land would *mourn* for the breaking of the covenant, just as it had mourned with drought during the wicked reign of King Ahab (see 1 Kings 17:1).

b. The leadership indicted for misleading the people (4:4-19). Just as a parent bears a tremendous responsibility before God to lead his children into the paths of righteousness (Prov. 22:6), so God's appointed leaders also are responsible to Him for the spiritual growth of those entrusted to them (cf. Acts 20:18-31; Phil. 1:5-7; Heb. 13:7, 17). In the case of Israel's downfall, the Lord holds the leadership responsible for leading the people down the broad road to destruction.

The fourth verse suggests that a contention had arisen as to who was at fault for the people's present predicament. In a strongly worded metaphor, Hosea likens those who are point-

2. In Hebrew, each of these commandments is stated by Hosea in the infinitive absolute, which is a grammatical form used to achieve vividness and emphasis. See William Rainey Harper, *A Critical and Exegetical Commentary on Amos and Hosea*, The International Critical Commentary, ed. Samuel Rolles Driver, Alfred Plummer, and Charles Augustus Briggs (Edinburgh: T. & T. Clark, 1905), p. 250.

ing the finger to "those who contend with the priest," an act forbidden by Mosaic law (in cases in which the priest sat as a judge) under penalty of death (Deut. 17:8-12). The leadership is corporately guilty, a certainty made plain by the change of address from "My people" to "your people." From verse 5, we can see that the major blame belongs to the priests (the pronoun "you" refers to the priests). But the verse also shows that the (false) prophets also have been guilty of causing the people to stumble. The pathetic scene of the prophets and priests of Ephraim reeling and staggering from strong drink while trying to render judgments is forcibly portrayed by Hosea's Judean contemporary Isaiah (Isa. 28:1-8). Blurred in vision by both a physical and a spiritual drunkenness, the priests and the prophets through their stumblings had become "blind guides of the blind" (Matt. 15:14). Because of that the Lord vows: "I will destroy your mother," a reference to the captivity that would befall the entire nation (see comment on 2:2).

The basic reason for this stern indictment is restated in verse 6 (cf. 4:1). The priests have failed to teach the people the life giving Word of God, and thus the people are "destroyed for lack of knowledge." For failing to accomplish their primary mission, the Lord rejects them from being His priests. Since the priesthood is customarily inherited, the Lord adds that He would forget (exclude) the children of the priest.[3]

From verses 4-6, one would expect that a decline in the knowledge of God had provoked a decline in the number of those joining the priesthood. However, verse 7 indicates that *both* the priesthood and sin were multiplying.[4] Hosea explains this strange phenomenon by stating that the priests encouraged the people to sin. This encouragement may be seen in two respects. First, the Hebrew word for *sin* (*chattath*) is the word for "sin offering," which was a biblical practice (Exod. 29:14; Lev. 4:3; Num. 6:11; Neh. 10:33) that had become idolatrous (1 Kings 12:28-33). It had become a sin to perform the sin offering.

3. Frederick Tatford, *Prophet of a Broken Home* (Sussex: Prophetic Witness, 1974), p. 58.
4. Differing from this view, Keil regards verse 7 as a reference to the increase in population, wealth, and prosperity that brought an attendant increase in sin. (C. F. Keil and F. Delitzsch, *Commentary on the Old Testament in Ten Volumes,* trans. James Martin [Grand Rapids: Eerdmans, n.d.], 10:78.)

Second, because their livelihood was derived through the sin offerings brought by the people, the priests were guilty of urging the people to sin (see Lev. 6:26). The more the people sinned, the more the priest prospered. Hosea's cry in verse 8, "They feed on the sin of my people," has been graphically translated, "They yearn for them with greedy throats."[5] So many cults today clamor with greedy throats for the money of their devotees, and give only false doctrine in return.

Verse 9's epigram, "like people, like priest," best describes the vicious cycle in which the priests and the people encouraged one another to descend lower and lower into sin. God warns the lust loving priests that both they and the people will be punished and fully repaid for their evil deeds. "Whatever a man sows, this he will also reap" (Gal. 6:7) is a basic principle that will be seen throughout the book of Hosea. This repayment for forsaking the Lord takes the form of insatiable hunger and fruitless wombs (v. 10), an irony because the worship of Baal was supposed to ensure the fertility of the soil and the fertility of the womb (cf. Deut. 31:17).

What happens to people who are led by those who have turned away from the knowledge of God? Verses 11-14 describe the debauchery. Priestly ceremonies involving "harlotry, wine, and new wine" had taken away the people's "understanding" or more literally, their "heart." In Hebrew thought, the heart stood for the seat of understanding (cf. 13:6), as well as the organ for reflective thinking (cf. 7:2, 11).[6] Addiction to harlotry or wine preoccupies the mind and takes away the understanding (v. 11).

As a substitute for *understanding*, verse 12 informs us that the people have chosen to be lead by a "spirit of harlotry," a force that the prophet perceives has driven them to perform foolish acts (cf. 5:14). As evidences of their folly, the prophet charges that the people have replaced the living God with a "wooden idol" (literally, "thing of wood") and a "diviner's wand"—neither of which have in them life or the ability to speak (cf. Isa. 44:9-20). Habakkuk's comment on this absurdity

5. Hans Walter Wolff, *Hosea*, trans. Gary Stansell, ed. Paul D. Hanson (Philadelphia: Westminster, 1969), p. 81.
6. E. B. Pusey, *The Minor Prophets: A Commentary* (Grand Rapids: Baker, 1950), 1:51.

is quite appropriate: "Woe to him who says to a piece of wood, 'Awake!'" (Hab. 2:19).

Another evidence of the spirit of harlotry was the very act of sacrificing to the gods of wood and stone (v. 13; cf. 2:13). By following the pagan customs of their neighbors, the Israelites rejected both God's appointed place of worship—Jerusalem—and the proper object of that worship—the Lord God (1 Kings 12: 26-29; 14:23; 2 Kings 17:10; Jer. 2:20).

If these transgressions were insufficient to prove the case, the Lord declares through Hosea that the spirit of harlotry had moved the leaders of Israel to allow daughters to play the harlot and brides to commit adultery (vv. 13b-14). By allowing their daughters to play the harlot, the Israelites willfully sinned against the Mosaic law that forbade the daughters of Israel from participating in the cult prostitution (Deut. 23:17). Because the word "brides" (Hebrew, *kallah*) literally means "daughters-in-law," Hosea may be alluding to the cultic practice of permitting a man to have sexual intercourse with his daughter-in-law to insure the fertility of her marriage.[7]

Reflecting on the results of the spirit of harlotry on His people, the Lord sighs: "So the people without understanding are ruined" (v. 14). *Ruined*, literally, "thrown down" (Hebrew, *labat*), is a word found elsewhere only in Proverbs 10:8, 10, where it describes the inevitable end of a fool who rejects God's commandments. In light of the scene that has been pictured in these verses, Israel has been "ruined" through her own folly.

With the example of Israel in ruin, the prophet turns for a moment to warn Judah not to follow in the same path of destruction (vv. 15-19). Like his predecessor Amos, the prophet Hosea warns the people of Judah not to enter Gilgal or Beth-aven (Bethel), cities considered to be heavily infected with idolatry (9:15; 12:11; Amos 4:4; 5:5). It should be noted that although a small town near Bethel did bear the name *Bethaven* in the time of Hosea, the parallel references in Amos (4:4; 5:5) force us to realize that Hosea is here contemptuously renaming "the house of God" (Bethel) as the "house of vanity" (Bethaven).

The fifteenth verse also contains a warning for Judah not to profane the name of the Lord as had been done by her cousins

7. James Luther Mays, *Hosea* (Philadelphia: Westminster, 1969), p. 75.

in Israel. Taking an oath by the name of the Lord was not forbidden (e.g., Judg. 8:19; Ruth 3:13; 1 Sam. 14:39; Jer. 38:16), but swearing by the Lord falsely in a place of idolatry was a sin because it associated the living God with idols (Lev. 19: 12; Zeph. 1:1-5).

The stubbornness of Israel, a subject well known to the beleaguered prophet, is described for Judah in verse 16 as a pattern that she dare not follow. Because of Israel's persistent obstinance, the nation is pictured as a "stubborn heifer" (cf. 10: 11), which cannot be pastured by the Lord. Frustrated by Israel's continual backsliding, Hosea cautions Judah: "Ephraim is joined to idols; let him alone" (v. 17). Ancient Hebrew commentators rendered the word *chabar* ("joined to") by terms such as "yoked to," "allied with," and "cleaving to," which strongly suggest the total merging that had occurred between Ephraim and idolatry.[8] The spirit of harlotry had done its work. Ephraim is married to idols (cf. Matt. 19:6 and its use of *joined*). Note that in this rebuke the prophet designates Israel by the name of its most dominant tribe, Ephraim. Since Ephraim was the tribe from which Jeroboam I came (1 Kings 11:26), the tribe became synonymous with the leadership in Israel. It seems that several of the thirty-seven references to Ephraim in Hosea designate particularly the guilty leadership that had led Israel (used 44 times) into apostasy (cf. 5:3, 5, 12-14; 6:10; 7:1, 8, 11; 9:8, 13; 12:1; 13:1).

The track record of Ephraim, the ruler of Israel, is stated for Judah's benefit in verses 18-19. Consumed by an insatiable desire for liquor and women, the rulers of Israel had brought shame upon the land. It is significant that the word *rulers* (Hebrew, *magen*) means literally "shields," which means the leadership should have been *shielding* God's people from wickedness. It is no less disheartening today to read that those commissioned "to shield" America are often found guilty of indulging in harlotry and the excessive consumption of liquor (cf. Prov. 16:12).

For all the shame that the leaders have caused, Hosea prophe-

8. J. J. Given, "Hosea." *The Pulpit Commentary*, ed. H. D. M. Spence and Joseph S. Exell. (Grand Rapids: Eerdmans, 1950), 13:106. *The Pulpit Commentary* is an excellent source for locating the opinions of ancient Hebrew and Christian scholars.

sies: "The wind wraps them in its wings" (v. 19). Wind (Hebrew, *ruach*) is a perfect figure for the sudden and violent judgment that will sweep the helpless nation into captivity. While in the midst of that captivity, men will see the folly of their sacrifices (4:13-14) and truly "be ashamed" (Hebrew, *bosh;* "become pale").

2. *The inevitability of judgment* (5:1-14)

When a warning is given, there is a natural tendency for us to deny that it could ever happen to us. Persons who have escaped from Eastern Europe have reported that they firmly believed Communism would never sweep over their land. "It can't happen here!" is the slogan of the fool. Israel had tuned out all prophets of doom, and thus the indictment of chapter 4 had gone unheeded by both people and leadership. Accordingly, Hosea proceeds in the fifth chapter with a proclamation that the announced judgment is *inevitable*.

a. Inevitable because of Israel's harlotry (5:1-7). "Hear," "Give heed," and "Listen" are the imperative watchwords by which the prophet hopes to alert the priests, the people ("house of Israel"), and the politicians ("house of the king") that the judgment of captivity applies to them. The definite article in Hebrew is prefixed to the word *judgment* (Hebrew, *mishpat*), which makes it all the more certain that the judgment about to fall upon Israel is that which was promised if the covenant was broken (Lev. 26:14-46; Deut. 28:15-68). Hosea's main target of attack is once again the leadership (specifically the priests), who have been guilty of ensnaring and netting the people in sin. None of the rebellious escape God's chastising hand (v. 2), for all have been a party to the nation's downfall. But even in this dark scene, the mercy of God shines through in the very word *chastise* (Hebrew, *musar*), which means "instruction with a view to ultimate redemption" (Deut. 11:2; Isa. 53:5; Jer. 30:14; cf. Heb. 12:8).

In verses 3-7, Hosea once again discloses that Ephraim is inhabited by a "spirit of harlotry" (see comment on 4:12). While in the fourth chapter the spirit of harlotry drove Israel away from the Lord, that same spirit is seen in chapter 5 to be the reason the Lord must withdraw from His people. The spirit of harlotry incited Ephraim's harlotry (v. 3; cf. 1:2; 4:4,

14; 7:4; 9:1); her evil deeds (v. 4; cf. 4:9; 7:2; 9:15; 12:2); her lack of the knowledge of the Lord (v. 4; cf. 4:1, 6, 14; 6:6); her misplaced pride (v. 5; cf. 7:10; Amos 8:7);[9] and all her iniquity (v. 5; cf. 4:8; 7:1, 15; 8:13; 9:7, 9; 13:12; 14:1-2). The Lord, who can say like a husband, "I know Ephraim" (cf. Gen. 4:1, 25), must *testify against* (cf. Ruth 1:21) and *withdraw* from His people. Israel's revelry in the spirit of harlotry had cost her the freedom to find God (v. 6). Sin had crowded God out of the lives of His own chosen people. This crowding out was evident in the new moon festivals, which Ephraim loved and God hated (v. 7; Isa. 1:14). The thought of the new moon devouring Ephraim has been paraphrased by Keil in this way: "Your sacrificial feast, your hypocritical worship, so far from bringing you salvation, will rather prove your ruin."[10]

b. Inevitable because of God's holiness (5:8-14). In verses 8-14 Hosea furnishes the people of his stiffnecked audience with a glimpse of the doom that would soon befall them at the hands of Assyria. The sounding of the ram's horn (Hebrew, *shophar*) and the blowing of the trumpet (Hebrew, *hatzotzerah*) were the standard warning systems that alerted the citizenry working in the fields to gather behind the city walls and prepare for battle (8:1; cf. Jer. 4:5; 6:1; Joel 2:1; Amos 3:6). The historical battle for which they were to prepare was the Syro-Ephraimite War (735-733 B.C.), in which the alliance of Rezin of Syria and Pekah of Israel captured certain Benjamite border towns, such as Gibeah, Ramah, and Bethel, or Beth-aven (see comment on 4:15; 2 Kings 16:5; Isa. 7:1-9). That action prompted Judah's King Ahaz to seek the aid of Assyria, the nation that then used Ahaz's request as a pretext to sweep down upon Syria (734 B.C.) and Israel (732 B.C.). Heartened by the aid received from Assyria, the people of Judah, using the old war cry "Behind you, Benjamin" (cf. Judg. 5:14), recaptured Gilgal, Ramah, and Bethel (v. 8).[11] To prevent any of the participants

9. As Amos 8:7 makes clear, the Lord was the pride of Israel. Israel had willfully permitted pride in her own accomplishments to replace the pride she should have had in the Lord. Thus the Lord, the pride of Israel, testifies against her. Harper, p. 270, disagrees with this view and sees Israel's arrogance as the "pride of Israel" that testifies against them.

10. Keil and Delitzsch, 10:89.

11. T. Miles Bennett, *Hosea: Prophet of God's Love* (Grand Rapids: Baker, 1975), pp. 65-66.

in that international intrigue from regarding themselves as being in charge of their own destiny, the Lord reminds them that it is He who declares "what is sure" (v. 9). Ephraim's initial aggression against Judah has resulted in "desolation in the day of rebuke" for the aggressor. Although God's holiness is vindicated in Ephraim's day of rebuke, His love and mercy are again seen (cf. 5:2) in the word *rebuke* (Hebrew, *tokechah*; literally, "reproof, correction"), which signifies discipline with the goal of restoration.

So that Judah would not come under the impression that God would defend only her, the Lord warns the Southern Kingdom that its retaliatory attack upon Ephraim (v. 8) is like the crime of moving a boundary line, an act forbidden under the penalty of a divine curse (Deut. 19:14; 27:17; for an historical incident of moving a boundary, see 1 Kings 15:22). For her crime, Judah will experience the wrath of God poured out upon her like a flood of water. *Wrath*, from a root word meaning "to run over," is especially appropriate as a figure for an overflowing, irresistible flood of judgment, something that the whole world will experience when the seven angels "pour out the seven bowls of the wrath of God into the earth" (Rev. 16:1).

In verse 11 the Lord returns again to the judgment that was soon to fall upon Ephraim, and He promises that Ephraim will be "oppressed" and "crushed in judgment," the exact punishment that Moses threatened if the people turned away from the Lord (Deut. 28:33). The reason for this judgment is based upon Ephraim's decision to follow the command of a man, possibly a reference to the command of Jeroboam I to worship the golden calves (1 Kings 12:28-33). In the hour of judgment the Lord, according to verse 12, has become "like a moth to Ephraim," secretly destroying the political fabric (stability) of the land (cf. Job 13:28). In like imagery, the Lord has become "like rottenness" to Judah, eating away the foundation of the royal house (cf. Isa. 40:20). Ephraim's immediate response was to seek human aid from Assyria's King Jareb (literally, "warrior king," a possible epithet for Tiglath-pileser III), rather than to fall on her knees before the Lord (v. 13). Like so many today, Ephraim's leaders trusted in chariots and horses, rather than the Lord, for deliverance (Psalm 20:7 [KJV]; see comment on 14:3).

Because she turned to Assyria, the Lord will make Himself like a lion (Hebrew, *shachal*) to Ephraim, which will prove once and for all His superior strength (cf. 13:7). Judah also will experience this tearing to pieces, but perhaps in a more gentle manner (see 2 Kings 18:13-16; 19:1-7), because "a young lion" (Hebrew, *kephir*) is known more for his roar than for his savagery (Job 4:10; Psalm 104:21; Isa. 31:4; Zech. 11:3).[12]

Just as He predicted, there was "none to deliver" when Ephraim's "ally" Assyria deported her people (v. 14; 2 Kings 15:29; 17:1-6) and nearly overran all of Judah (2 Kings 18:13-16). How quickly Israel had forgotten the words of the psalmist: "Salvation belongs to the LORD" (Psalm 3:8).

3. The necessity of complete repentance (5:15–6:3)

Continuing his policy of tempering severe sections on judgment with a message of hope (1:10–2:1; 2:14-23; 3:5), Hosea promises in the fifteenth verse that the Lord will return to the people when they acknowledge their guilt and earnestly seek Him. Unfortunately, millennia of future suffering fall between the last verse of the fifth chapter and the first verse of chapter 6. In the first three verses of this sixth chapter, Hosea voices the cry that he wishes his own generation would articulate, but that will remain unuttered until the Lord Himself steps upon the Mount of Olives (Zech. 12:10; 14:1-4). In the words "He has torn us, but He will heal us," Israel finally comes to the realization that her sufferings have been of a disciplinary nature.[13]

The confident assertion of the people, "He will raise us up on the third day" (v. 2), does not contextually speak of the resur-

---

12. Jack B. Scott, *The Book of Hosea* (Grand Rapids: Baker, 1971), p. 44.
13. An alternate interpretation aligns verses 1-3 with verse 4 of chapter 6 and asserts that the repentance expressed is *superficial* because of a number of factors, including the lack of any mention of a genuine contrition for sin. Arguments favoring this view are to be found in D. David Garland, *Hosea* (Grand Rapids: Zondervan, 1975), p. 48. The view chosen here is also that of Keil, who notes that Hosea's style involves the use of rapid transitions (compare 2:1 and 2:2). Rather than aligning 6:1-3 with 6:4, the first three verses of chapter 6 are to be seen as the cry of the repentant nation that is finally seeking the Lord in time of affliction (5:15). For further study, see Keil and Delitzsch, 10:96.

rection of Christ, but rather the sudden resurrection of Israel
when she repents (Ezek. 37). The resurrection of Israel will
trigger a renewed interest in the knowledge of the Lord, which
she will have shamefully rejected for so many centuries (4:6).
The Lord's coming to revive Israel in that day is as assured as
the divine decree that the dawn must follow the night (Gen.
8:22). Furthermore, the coming of the Lord will be like the
latter (spring) rain, always an occasion for rejoicing because
of the benefit that is given to the crops (Deut. 11:14; Job 29:23;
Prov. 16:15; Joel 2:23).

4. *The impossibility of immediate restoration* (6:4–7:16)

a. Impossible because of Israel's lack of loyalty (6:4-11).
Hosea, knowing of the glorious future that awaited a repentant
Israel, shared fully in the Lord's frustration, as expressed in the
inquiry of verse 4, "What shall I do with you, O Ephraim?"
Israel's chronic ailment, disloyalty, was easy to diagnose but
so difficult to remedy because of her strong resistance as a
patient. A dizzying cyclical pattern of loyalty—disloyalty—
punishment had become ingrained in Israel's character since
the time of the judges (e.g., Judg. 4:1-24). Now, however, the
malignancy of disloyalty had spread throughout the nation,
causing the temporary remedies to become obsolete. Drastic
action was a necessity.

As metaphors of Israel's loyalty, the Lord chose the morning
cloud and the dew, figures expressing something that has
beauty but no substance. The people who have no inner substance need the life of God infused into them.[14] The Lord Jesus
Christ, God in the flesh, is still the only hope for Israel. But
the people of Israel in Hosea's day were not left without a witness to the coming of Christ, for the Lord commissioned an
array of prophets to wield the Word of God like a powerful
weapon (Isa. 49:2; Jer. 5:14; 23:29; cf. Eph. 6:17; Heb. 4:12).
The Lord also showed Israel her proper and lawful conduct by
the judgments that the prophets and priests rendered (v. 5).
In both judgment and hope, Israel was sufficiently informed.

14. For an excellent essay on the use of the metaphors of the morning
    cloud and the dew as expressions of the loyalty of Israel, consult
    G. Campbell Morgan, *Hosea: The Heart and Holiness of God* (Grand
    Rapids: Baker, 1974), pp. 60-69.

Turning to the sacrificial system that was employed in Israel, the Lord in verse 6 laments that Israel's sacrifices are meaningless without a corresponding loyalty (Hebrew, *chesed*) to the One to whom those sacrifices were directed (see also 1 Sam. 15:22; Jer. 7:22-23; Mic. 6:6-8). How easy it is for Christians today to sing "I Surrender All" on Sunday morning, knowing full well that they will dedicate the rest of the week to fulfilling their own self-centered interests. Hosea is not by any means advocating the extinguishing of ceremonial worship, but rather is simply saying that without a heart love for God all burnt offerings are meaningless (v. 6; cited by the Lord in Matt. 9:13; 12:7).

To prove that sacrifices and offerings made to God without a desire to love Him or know Him more are worthless, Hosea in verses 7-9 reviews the evidence from three of Israel's cities. The identification of the first town, Adam, has been the subject of much dispute. It is argued by some that the reference is not to a town, but rather to the first man to break a covenant with God—Adam.[15] However, the context of verses 8-9, where towns are mentioned, strongly suggests that Adam is the name of a town. Identified in Scripture as the site where the waters of the Jordan divided (Josh. 3:16), Adam had fallen like the rest of Israel in transgressing the covenant.[16] Gilead is singled out in the next verse as a city where murder reigned and covenant obligations were ignored. Both Gilead (Ramoth Gilead, Josh. 21:38) and Shechem (Josh. 21:21) were "cities of refuge," and yet both had become cities of unrestrained sin. Unlike the people of Gilead, the citizens of Shechem are not condemned, but rather a band of murdering priests is condemned, a group that had been terrorizing those trying to enter Shechem. Speaking of this evil band, the Lord avows: "Surely they have committed crime." Light concerning the nature of that crime may be discerned by an examination of the word *crime* (Hebrew, *zimmah*), which has special reference to "crimes of immorality" (cf. Lev. 18:17; 19:29; 20:14; Judg. 20:6; Job 31:11). Guilty of both murder and immorality, the priests near Shechem symbolized the extent of the depravity of a people that forgot God. According to verse 11, that wickedness also was rampant in

15. Laetsch, p. 61.
16. Bennett, p. 71.

Judah, a fact that would necessitate that a harvest of judgment take place there as well (Jer. 51:33; Joel 3:12). When those judgments are completed, a convicted and purged nation will once more be deserving of the title "My people" (Hebrew, *ammi*).

b. Impossible because of Israel's secret sins (7:1-7). The lack of loyalty to the Lord already has been proved as a reason that an immediate restoration of the nation is impossible (6:4-11). Now, in the first seven verses of chapter 7, the Lord adds a second reason for the impossibility of immediate restoration: the continual revelation of unconfessed secret sins. Without a full and complete judgment for sin, the holiness of God will continue to expose sin and foil any attempts to restore the nation. If it were not for the full payment for sin made upon Calvary, we too would stand eternally unacceptable to God (1 Pet. 3:18).

Israel's chronic ailment, disloyalty to God, had spread like a cancer into the social and political systems of the land. From verses 1-3 we can observe that the whole kingdom was "living a lie." Israelite society enjoyed an early version of the "new morality," encouraged political corruption, and winked at the rising crime rate. But there was a tragic flaw in all that—the people did not consider in their hearts that a holy God remembered all their wickedness (v. 2; Psalm 14:2-4; 50:21). With their excuse, "Everybody's doing it," the people of Hosea's day had mistakenly thought that standards of right and wrong should be judged by that which was the accepted practice. When our society considers legalizing marijuana, are we listening to the facts or to the cry, "Everybody's doing it!"? The one thing forgotten in both Hosea's day and our own is that God's standards and the penalties inherent in the breaking of those standards do not change.

The effect that the breakdown in religious and moral standards had on the political structure of the land is delineated in verses 3-7. Rather than rising above the tumult of wickedness, the king and his princes (military advisers) were willing participants in the thrill of "doing their own thing." In verse 4, Hosea compares the release of all moral restraints to the heating up of leavened bread in the oven. The fuel for that heat is labeled as wine (Hebrew, *yayin*), the agent already blamed for taking away the understanding of the people (cf. 4:11). When that wine has heated up its imbiber to the point of a frenzied climax, it results in the consuming (through assassination) of the rulers (vv. 5-6). In verse 7, Hosea wails, "All their kings have fallen," a reference not only to the murders of Zechariah, Shallum, Pekahiah, and Pekah, but also to the disastrous reign of Menahem (who allowed Israel to become a vassal of Assyria, 2 Kings 15:19), and prophetically to Hoshea (who was soon to be imprisoned by Assyria, 2 Kings 17:4). Is wine still a consuming heat today? The answer can be found on the front page of your local newspaper almost every day of the week.

c. Impossible because of Israel's dependence upon other nations for security (7:8-16). In verses 8-16, Hosea furnishes the third reason that immediate restoration for Israel is an impossibility—Israel's dependence on Assyria and Egypt for security. In the wilderness God commanded His chosen nation to remain separate from other nations because of the inevitable contamination that would otherwise result (Num. 23:9; Deut. 33:28). Through continued disloyalty to God, Ephraim had mixed herself with other nations, hoping those nations would provide the security that God had already promised. Ephraim's disloyalty prompted the Lord in verse 8 to describe the nation as a "cake not turned." An unturned or half-baked cake is useless because it is burned on one side and uncooked on the other. Because she failed to fulfill her appointed destiny, Ephraim's misplaced trust marked the nation as useless to God.

In addition to making Ephraim useless to God, the mixing with the nations had induced a depletion of the strength of Israel (v. 9). Indeed, Ephraim suffered financially from the tributes that were paid to Assyria (2 Kings 15:19-20) and from the costly Syro-Ephraimite War, in which she allied with Syria (Isa. 7:2). Hosea likens Ephraim to a man who has unwittingly become prematurely gray through constant dissipation. All the warning signs of demise are present "yet he does not know it" (v. 9). Even the testimony of the Lord God, the "pride of Israel" (see note on 5:5), could not provoke the apostate nation to reverse her course and seek the Lord.

In verses 10-11, Hosea moves from a general condemnation of Ephraim's foreign policy to a specific example of how that policy was leading the nation to the brink of disaster. Ephraim is likened to "a silly dove"—one that flies uncertainly to and fro, displaying no loyalty. In asserting that the dove is "without sense" (literally, "heart"), Hosea reinforces the concept that Ephraim had no real heart love for her divine benefactor. The true senselessness of her foreign policy is shown by Ephraim's crying out to her natural enemies Egypt and Assyria in times of distress. An historical example of that occurred during the time of Pekah, who went to Egypt for assistance while under the vassalship of Assyria. For his disloyalty to Assyria, Pekah lost both his country and his life (2 Kings 15:29-30).

As is announced in verse 12, Ephraim's freedom to pursue the help of other nations was fast coming to an end. With Ephraim securely trapped in God's net, the Lord finally would be able to "chastise them in accordance with the proclamation to their assembly" (v. 12). Again, the word *chastise* (Hebrew, *yasar*) speaks of the loving instruction of a parent for his child (Deut. 8:5; Prov. 19:18; 29:17; cf. Heb. 12:5, 7). This proclamation may refer to the various warnings by the prophets, but it is more likely that the reference is primarily directed to the giving of the law in Deuteronomy (Deut. 28:15-68).[17]

Because the law was given by Moses, Israel had always possessed the knowledge of the two ways: redemption or rebellion (cf. Deut. 32). Verse 13 rehearses the Lord's utter chagrin that Israel has strayed, rebelled, and spoken lies against Him. For the people's transgressions the Lord pronounces upon them a "woe" (Hebrew, *oy*), normally a word reserved for the introduction of judgment upon heathen nations (Num. 21:29; Isa. 3:11; Jer. 48:46; cf. Matt. 11:21; Rev. 8:13). Such a woe was well deserved—Israel's treachery had rejected God's proffered redemption. The word *redeem* (Hebrew, *pada*) is a term of commercial law that refers to the reclaiming or ransoming of an obligated person by means of a payment. God exercised His ransoming power when He redeemed Israel from Egypt (Exod. 15:13), and according to Hosea 13:14 God's intervention will one day effect a full redemption for the nation.[18]

An example of the lies that foiled Israel's redemption in Hosea's day is found in verse 14. The Lord through the voice

17. Pusey, 1:76.
18. Mays, p. 111.

of the prophet charges that the Israelites pretended to worship the Lord, when all the while their hearts belonged to their idols. Their mistaken belief that Baal gave them the grain and new wine led them to the fatal error of turning away from the Lord (cf. 2:5, 8, 12).

The indictment against Israel closes with a few broken lines that fall on the page like tears from one with a broken heart (vv. 15-16). No matter how hard the Lord tried to train (literally, "discipline") and strengthen Israel for her battle against wickedness, she rejected Him by joining the side of evil. She had become "like a deceitful bow," failing the archer in the time of battle. Without the Lord, who was her strength (Psalm 28:7), Israel would fall helplessly prostrate at the feet of her captors.

4

GOD'S JUSTICE PUNISHES ISRAEL

B. GOD'S JUSTICE PUNISHES AN UNREPENTANT ISRAEL (8:1—10:15)

1. *The necessity of judgment* (8:1-4)

With the indictment fully stated, no one in Hosea's day could logically deny the necessity of punishment for the wayward nation. God's justice had to be vindicated (Deut. 28:15-68). Israel had sown the wind, and she would now reap the whirlwind (8:7).

a. God's goodness rejected (8:1-3). In the eighth chapter, Hosea launches immediately into an announcement of the judgment that is to befall the nation. A trumpet (cf. 5:8) is again sounded to warn the nation that the judgment is about to commence. Assyria, pictured as a swift eagle (Deut. 28:49), has been designated as God's tool to render justice for the transgressing of the covenant. Historically, this prediction of judgment was fulfilled both in the invasion of Tiglath-pileser III (734-733 B.C.), and in the conquest of Shalmaneser in 722 B.C. (2 Kings 15:29; 17:1-6). With the enemy approaching, Israel makes a last ditch attempt to assuage the wrath of God with the cry ,"My God, we of Israel know Thee!" (v. 2). Pious words without a backing from a changed heart could not reverse the planned judgment. Israel could not have truly known God, because she had rejected "the good" (v. 3). The good (Hebrew, *tob*) is a reference not only to God's character (Amos 5:14; Mic. 6:8); but also to the manifestation of His goodness in covenant blessings (2:8; 3:5). As proof that Israel has rejected the good, Hosea devotes the remainder of the chapter to the enumeration of specific examples of Israel's folly.

b. God's sovereignty rejected (8:4). Hosea begins the list of rejections of God with that which truly precipitated all the rest—the division of the monarchy by Jeroboam I (1 Kings 12:

19-20). After he removed Israel from the control of God's appointed ruling house (2 Sam. 7:13, 16), Jeroboam I instituted a monarchy that would witness the violent rise and fall of ten dynasties in a relatively short two hundred years. Whereas political instability was a by-product of Israel's choosing her own kings, the major result of that separation from God's authority was the establishment of idolatry in the land. The making of idols, strictly forbidden by the law (Exod. 20:3-6; 34:17; Lev. 19:4), was inaugurated by Jeroboam I at Dan and Bethel (1 Kings 12:28-31).

c. God's worship rejected (8:5-7). Jeroboam I had deviously taught the people that they were still worshiping the Lord when they bowed before the idols. The Lord now vents His anger against those who pay homage to the calf of Samaria. Aware that the calf was made by a craftsman, Israel stood without excuse. They should have known that "it is not God" (v. 6). No other nation on the face of the earth had been entrusted with the knowledge of God (Gen. 32:28; Exod. 19:4-6), and yet Israel had traded the knowledge of the truth for a lie. In case there was still a glimmer of hope that deliverance would come through the calf, Hosea prophesies that the calf "will be broken to pieces," symbolizing the calf's inability to deliver itself, much less the people. With the knowledge of God we have in our hearts, do we ever take time to examine whether we have let any "golden calves" usurp the position that God should have in our lives?

Verse 7 climaxes the condemnation for not worshiping God with a promise that Israel would suffer greatly for her sins. The two centuries that Israel sowed the wind have yielded two millennia in which she has reaped the whirlwind (cf. 9:17). The divine law of the harvest will be meted out (10:13; 12:2; Job 4:8; Gal. 6:7). Israel finally would learn that God is a *God of justice*, who rules a moral universe in which sin has its natural consequences that must be paid. In reflecting on this passage, Kyle Yates has affirmed: "Unforeseen terrors are in store for the one who has carelessly plunged into sin."[19]

d. God's omnipotence rejected (8:8-10). A third cause for judgment is traced in verses 8-10 to the refusal of Israel to trust

19. Kyle M. Yates, *Preaching from the Prophets* (Nashville: Broadman, 1942), p. 77.

in God for protection. Israel, designed by God to be separate
from the world (Exod. 19:5; Deut. 10:15; 14:2), had become so
swallowed up in the manners and beliefs of her neighbors that
she finally loses the reason for her existence (v. 8). Finding
international politics to be a treacherous game, Israel turns for
asylum to her strongest enemy, Assyria. Israel's stubbornness,
likened to that of a wild donkey, does not permit her to choose
God in her crisis (v. 9). In the hope that such alliances would
enable her to obtain wealth, political power, and prestige,
Israel seeks hired lovers by creating alliances with heathen
nations. There is no thought for the spiritual benefit of her
new heathen allies; the "profit motive" is her only interest.

Israel's search for power and wealth will come to a grinding
halt when God gathers the people back to the nation for judgment. With Assyria claiming more territory and more taxes as
each year passed, Hosea's contemporaries could not honestly
deny that Israel had begun "to diminish" (literally, "to sorrow
awhile, to suffer awhile"). Although the imposition of tribute
on the people had led to "suffering for awhile," a greater suffering was soon coming in the form of captivity.[20]

e. God's commandments rejected (8:11-14). The Lord God
in the Torah (Pentateuch) has dispensed explicit commands
regarding every phase of life, and through each of those commandments the people were to learn more about the character
of their Maker. These "ten thousand precepts," a reference to
the completeness of this revelation from God, were regarded
"as a strange [unknown] thing" by the Israelites (v. 12). The
most glaring example of that willful ignorance was the way the
leaders of Israel contemptuously trampled on God's command
that sacrifices be made only from the site He revealed to them
(Deut. 12:13-14; cf. 1 Kings 8:13). Rather than worshiping the
Lord at the appointed place, Ephraim sinned by worshiping
idols at various improper sites (v. 11). If that was not enough
to condemn the nation to God's judgment, Hosea notes that
the priests who performed the sacrifices thought only of the
personal benefit that would come to them as they exercised their
sacerdotal duties (v. 13). The Lord takes no delight (Hebrew,

20. Robert Jamieson, A. R. Fausset, and David Brown, *A Commentary,
    Critical and Explanatory, on the Old and New Testaments* (Grand
    Rapids: Eerdmans, n.d.), 2:486.

ratsah) in such sacrifices, just as He is displeased with those today who amass great personal fortunes under the pretext of preaching the gospel. For Israel, her obstinance and opportunism would lead her back into bondage—a threat that was encroaching upon the nation even as Hosea preached.

In the fourteenth verse, Hosea closes chapter 8 with a brief analysis of the basic reason for Israel's punishment. After following their own way for two hundred years, the people of the Northern Kingdom had completely lost track of God. How could Israel forget her Maker? The preventatives and warnings against such forgetfulness were spelled out in great detail in the book of Deuteronomy (Deut. 8:19; cf. Deut. 4:9, 23, 31; 6:12; 8:11, 14; 9:7; 24:19; 25:19). Nevertheless, Israel had become "the land of forgetfulness" (Psalm 88:12), and for this they would be consumed by God's wrath. As verse 14 also reveals, Israel was not alone in this sin; Judah also had caught the infection of forgetfulness. Judah's multiplication of fortified cities meant a switch from trusting in God to trusting in herself. For falling into the same sin as her sister Israel, Judah's cities would be consumed, a threat fulfilled when Sennacherib destroyed all of Judah's fortified cities except Jerusalem (2 Kings 18:13—19:35).

2. *The nature of judgment* (9:1—10:15)

After sowing the wind for two centuries, the nation of Israel is granted in chapters 9-10 a glimpse of the whirlwind that will sweep her into judgment. As will be observed throughout this section, God's judgment in each case is a particular fulfillment of the sowing-reaping principle (cf. Gal. 6:8). Those sins that Israel sowed have become the seeds of her well-deserved judgment.

a. Judgment brings sorrow (9:1-2). In this first judgment—the failure of the harvest—God grants Israel's desire to be dependent totally upon the blessings of the Baalim she worshiped. Such a judgment verified the folly of attributing to idols that which had been bestowed by Almighty God. Israel rejoiced "with exultation like the nations" when she partook of the harvest festivals that had become laced with idolatry and immorality. That rejoicing, Hosea warns, must come to an end. The harvest will fail.

b. Judgment brings exile (9:3-9). In order to bring stability to the nation, the leaders of Ephraim turned for help to their neighbors (Assyria and Egypt) rather than to God. Because Ephraim had "sowed" a fondness for mixing with her neighbors, the Lord arranged for her to enjoy those pleasures on a "full time" basis—in exile. In stating that Ephraim "will return to Egypt," Hosea is primarily alluding to the fact that Israel had proved herself unworthy of the freedom she had enjoyed in the land of Palestine. Moses had commanded the people never to return to Egypt, a law they had transgressed frequently (see comment on 14:3; cf. Deut. 17:16). Egypt represented *bondage* (Exod. 20:2), and it is in that sense that the word *Egypt* is to be interpreted. Israel's bondage would take place in a land far worse than Egypt, the land of Assyria. In Assyria, the Israelites would reap the deserved reward for ignoring God's law in regard to dietary regulations—"they will eat unclean food" (v. 3). Before the eyes of God, all the food that Israel had consumed had been unclean, because she had failed to present to God the firstfruits of each food (cf. Exod. 22:29; 23:19; 34:22-26; Lev. 23:10-17).[21]

The ramifications of living in uncleanness are envisioned in verses 4-5. Israel had not truly been sacrificing to the Lord in her own homeland, and therefore she will endure the penalty of knowing that all sacrifices offered in a foreign land will be void of any meaning (v. 4). As Charles Feinberg has commented, Israel is this hour still suffering the predicament of verse 4, "not pleasing to God, because the reconciliation brought about through Christ's sacrifice she has not yet received by faith. (See Ro. 10:1-4.)"[22]

For a nation that still is deprived of sacrifices the festival days, according to verse 5, become times of gloom and sorrow. The effect on Israel during her feast days would be comparable to the grief felt by a parent on the birthday of a recently deceased child. The sorrows of captivity will also extend to include the loss of all the Israelites' material possessions (v. 6).

Verses 7-9 further intensify the swiftness and immediacy of judgment. Hosea tersely warns his audience that the "days of

21. Laetsch, p. 73.
22. Charles L. Feinberg, *The Minor Prophets* (Chicago: Moody, 1977), p. 45.

punishment" and "days of retribution" have indeed come. Blind to the fact that God has brought the Assyrians to judge them for their sins (5:13-14; 7:9-10), the Israelites continue to wallow in their iniquity. Commentators have disagreed over who is speaking these words, found in verse 7: "The prophet is a fool, the inspired man is demented." If this is Hosea, then these words are a condemnation of the false prophets. On the other hand, these words may be the people's reaction to the ministry of Hosea. By reproducing the thoughts of his contemporaries, Hosea would be offering us a glimpse of the opposition that he faced as he proclaimed the Word of the Lord.[23] Although weighty arguments have been adduced for both viewpoints, it seems more appropriate to render these verses as a further condemnation of Ephraim's false leadership. Motivated by a "deceiving spirit" (1 Kings 22:22), the prophet who tells Israel to be at ease is labeled by Hosea as a "fool" (cf. Psalm 107:17; Prov. 1:7; Isa. 19:11; 35:8). "The inspired man" (Hebrew, *ish haruach* is a somewhat unfavorable synonym for prophet and is based on a play on the word *spirit* (Hebrew, *ruach*), which could also be translated "wind." (Jeremiah 5:13 is an example of such a play on words.) The words of the false prophet are as lacking in substance as the wind. Such a prophet is likewise *demented* (Hebrew, *meshugga*), a word that also was used to describe David's pretended insanity before Achish of Gath (1 Sam. 21:12-14; cf. Deut. 28:34; 2 Kings 9:11; Jer. 29:26). The fruits of their labor in Israel are described as "iniquity" and "hostility." Hostility (Hebrew, *mastemah*), which comes from the verb root *staman* (literally, "to bear a grudge"), had been encouraged by the false prophets who caused the people to bear a grudge against God and His true prophets.[24]

In contrast to what Ephraim's prophets had become, Hosea looks into the past in verse 8 and declares, "Ephraim was a watchman with my God, a prophet." True prophets were God's *watchmen* (Hebrew, *tsaphah*; literally, "look out"), carrying out the work of guarding the nation from all dangers (Isa. 52:8; Jer. 6:17; Ezek. 3:17; Mic. 7:4; Hab. 2:1). Rather than guarding the nation from evil, the prophets of Israel, according to Hosea, have snared the people into performing wickedness

23. Mays, p. 129.
24. Keil and Delitzsch, 10:123.

(Isa. 56:10). Their shameful activities are likened to "the days of Gibeah," a reference to that time in Israel's past when all but six hundred of the men of Benjamin were killed in an act of genocide. This had been triggered by the depravity of the men of Gibeah (Benjamites) toward the concubine of a Levite (Judg. 19:13–20:48). Even as the Lord brought a severe punishment for iniquity at that time, so also will He now remember the iniquity and hostility of Ephraim and render her a punishment befitting her sins. Exile and oblivion await.

c. Judgment brings death (9:10-17). The heartbreak of being taken from one's homeland is compounded in verses 10-17 by the revelation that the exile will be accompanied by death. This announcement is interspersed with three flashbacks that probe Israel's past (vv. 10*a*, 10*b*, 15). The first of these flashbacks recalls the joy that was experienced by the Lord when He first found Israel and brought her into the wilderness. The Lord's joy is likened both to that of a hungry traveler who finds grapes growing in the desert, and to that joy of a gardener who finds the first ripe fruit of the season on his fig tree. Both metaphors point to the belief that great things would come from this new find—a prospect that would soon be dispelled. This same movement from joy to despair is found in the Song of Moses (Deut. 32). Both Moses and Hosea disclose the treacherous way in which the people of Israel abused the love of God, and both announce that such idolatry and harlotry will be punished by exile and death (Deut. 32:15-42).

In order once again to offer a reason for judgment, the Lord looks back to a "trend setting" historical precedent for Israel's infidelity (v. 10*b*). The flashback to Baal-peor is a reference to the time when Israel first corrupted herself by committing adultery with the Moabites and devoting herself to their idols (Num. 25:1-9). The Lord labels the Israelites' depraved conduct at Baal-peor with the word *shame* (Hebrew, *bosheth*), which is the same term used to describe the effect of Baalism on the land of Israel (Jer. 11:13). Just as God punished with death those who participated in the lewd practices at Baal-peor, so God will punish with death the nation as a whole for her physical and spiritual adultery.

In the context of the eleventh verse, Israel's glory (Hebrew, *kabod*) is the children of the Israelites, those whom the people believed would continue to live and prosper in the land. The great irony would be that Ephraim, whose name means "doubly fruitful" in Hebrew, would be barren. Again, the sowing-reaping principle comes into play as Ephraim receives the proper punishment for falsely crediting her fertility to Baal. Without God's blessing, which Ephraim did not seek, the people would quickly learn the fruitlessness of their fertility rites before gods who could not hear and answer.

According to verse 12, God's judgment of death will not only prevent the birth of new children, but will also include the death of those children already born in Israel when the judgment was announced. As was forewarned in Deuteronomy 32: 25, the death of living children will come through the ravages of war. A woe (see comment on 7:13) spelling ominous disaster awaits Israel when the Lord leaves them to the mercy of their impotent gods. As pictured in verse 13, the departure from the Lord means an exchange of a "pleasant meadow" (symbolizing peace) for a field filled with slaughtered children (symbolizing the destruction of war).

With such a heavy message of doom Hosea in verse 14 breaks forth into a prayer for the people. Deeply affected by the severity of judgment, Hosea asks, "What wilt Thou give?" Faced with an overwhelming record of ancient and modern apostasy, Hosea can only plead that future Israelite generations will not be born (v. 14). Although this petition sounds harsh, it is in a real sense a prayer for mercy—a prayer that new generations will not have to experience the trail of tears upon which Hosea's generation was about to embark.[25]

By yet another geography lesson on sin, verses 15-17 underscore the necessity of this punishment of death. Gilgal is chosen as the site where God "came to hate them," a reference to the depth of God's threat of judgment to the nation that refused to repent. In the eyes of the Lord Gilgal stood for both the historic rebellion against God, in the establishment of a human monarchy (1 Sam. 11:14-15; cf. 1 Sam. 8:7; Hos. 3:4; 7:3-7; 8:4; 10:3, 7, 15), and the current spiritual rebellion, in the establishment of a shrine to Baal (4:15; Amos 4:4; 5:5; cf.

25. In support of the view that would see this as an intercession for mercy on the part of Hosea, consult Wolff, pp. 166-67. Laetsch, p. 77, does not find a note of mercy in the request.

Hos. 12:4).[26] For Israel's wickedness, so capsulized in Gilgal's rejection of divine sovereignty and divine homage, the Lord vows, "I will drive them out of My house!" In Scripture the word *drive* (Hebrew, *garash*) possesses the force of a violent retribution for sin. (See Gen. 3:24; 4:14; 21:10; Exod. 6:1; 10:11; 23:28-32; 33:2; Num. 22:6, 11; Josh. 24:12, 18; Judg. 2:3; 6:9; 1 Sam. 26:19; 1 Chron. 17:21; Ezek. 31:11; Zeph. 2:4.) Excluding the references in Genesis, it should be noted that *garash* is used mainly to refer to the expulsion of the Canaanites out of the land of Palestine. Now, the Israelites are to be driven out.

In the book of Genesis, the word *garash* is employed in three dramatic scenes that parallel events recorded in the last few verses of this chapter of Hosea. The parallels begin with Adam and Eve, who were *driven out* of the Garden of Eden for their sin (Gen. 3:24). In like manner, Israel would be *driven out* of the "pleasant meadow" that God had planted for Ephraim (v. 13; cf. Gen. 2:8). A second parallel is to be found in the correspondence between verse 15 and the request of Sarah that Abraham would *drive out* Hagar and her son Ishmael (Gen. 21:10). Like Hosea's own son Lo-ammi ("not my people"), Israel would be *driven out* from the presence of God's love. As an outcast, Ephraim, the doubly fruitful plant, would dry up and bear no more fruit. She had tapped into the wrong source of nourishment and would therefore wither and die (v. 16). A final parallel use of *garash* may be found in the relation between verse 17 and the story of Cain in Genesis 4:14. Just as God *drove out* Cain from His presence and caused him to be a fugitive in the earth, so also God decreed that Israel would be *driven out* and "will be wanderers among the nations" (v. 17). As has been true in any generation, those today who fail to hearken unto the voice of the Lord will walk alone into the misery of eternal separation from God. Spiritual and physical death await such persons!

d. Judgment brings terror (10:1-15). The frightful predictions recorded in the tenth chapter bring to a close the section of Hosea that etches in the mind of the reader the *justice* of Almighty God. Israel's guilt and punishment are again in view in the first two verses. Whether the vine is "empty" (KJV) or "luxuriant" (NASB) is solved by a study of the Hebrew word

26. Bennett, p. 92.

boqeq, which comes from a root word *baqaq,* "to run luxuriantly, to overflow." Indeed, the blessings of the Lord in behalf of Israel "overflowed" as they created a "luxuriant vine" (cf. Psalm 80:8-11). Refusing to acknowledge that these blessings had come from God, Israel produced "fruit for himself" rather than for the Lord. Accordingly, the Lord decrees that their heart is "faithless" (Hebrew, *chalaq*; literally, "divided, smooth, trickish, treacherous"). A faithless or divided heart had long been Israel's tragic flaw. Elijah, a century earlier than Hosea, encountered this divided loyalty when he asked the people, "How long will you hesitate between two opinions?" (1 Kings 18:21). Even today, we need to be exhorted not to be "double-minded," for such an attitude leads to instability and ruin (James 1:8). Through the law, Israel had received a sense of what was right, but that sense was met by an overwhelming love for doing what was wrong. For choosing the bad, Hosea warns that the people will bear their own "guilt" (Hebrew, *asham*; used only here in the Old Testament).

When the Lord has broken down the altars and sacred pillars (v. 2), Samaria will finally realize that she has been caught. The people will exclaim, "We have no king," which will signify that none was worthy of the name *king* (v. 3).[27] Entrapment, however, does not provoke a repentance in Samaria, but rather a temporary sorrow that she has been caught (see the example of Judas, Matt. 27:3-4). Samaria's kings had attempted to make the nation secure by seeking alliances with Assyria and Egypt, but such actions were worthless because they served merely to nullify the only covenant that could protect them—that which God had granted at Sinai (Exod. 34:9-13). In being faithless to the Lord's promises for protection, Samaria sowed the seeds of her own judgment, which were now sprouting "like poisonous weeds" throughout the land (v. 4). While America still has In God We Trust on her coins, she has likewise deemed it expedient to make covenants with treacherous nations that despise the Lord.

With judgment choking Samaria to death, her first concern, according to verse 5, is for the capture of the calf of Beth-aven

27. Charles F. Pfeiffer, "Hosea," in *The Wycliffe Bible Commentary,* ed. Charles F. Pfeiffer and Everett F. Harrison (Chicago: Moody, 1962), p. 812.

(Bethel, see comment on 5:8). With her god in the hands of the enemy, "Ephraim will be seized with shame" (v. 6). Finally, she will realize her error in heeding the counsel of Jeroboam I to establish calf worship at Bethel (1 Kings 12:29). Securely in the hands of a just God, Israel would learn that she is powerless.

Do we need a deeper appreciation for the justice of God? When Jonathan Edwards preached his famous sermon "Sinners in the Hands of an Angry God" (1734), he prepared the way for the Great Awakening, which spread throughout the American colonies and resulted in the conversion of many. This same sermon, when studied by me in an American literature class some years ago, provoked only ridicule by the teacher and students. The justice of God, today as well as in Hosea's day, is lightly esteemed by a sin-loving people. As verse 7 predicts, Israel's light estimation of the warnings of God will result in her (and her king) being cut off and becoming like a stick floundering helplessly at the mercy of the tides.

The release of the judgment of God will create a state of terror in which the people of Israel will cry out for the mountains to cover them, and for the hills to fall upon them (v. 8). Seven hundred years later, the Lord Jesus utilized this same imagery to predict the reaction of the Jews to their destruction by Rome in A.D. 70 (Luke 23:30). In addition to this example, those in the Great Tribulation, who experience the terror of the sixth seal, will likewise cry out for the mountains to fall on them (Rev. 6:16).

Another parallel between the time of the fall of Samaria and the time of the Great Tribulation may be deduced by noting the similar condition of the respective groups to be judged by God. The phrase in verse 9, "the days of Gibeah" (see comment on 9:9), parallels the New Testament concept of "the days of Noah" (Matt. 24:37; cf. 2 Pet. 2:5) in the sense that both speak of a period of unrestrained wickedness. Thus Hosea warns that the whole nation is standing like Gibeah of old, in a position that demands the judgment of God. The tenth verse amplifies the threat as God announces that "the peoples" (foreign invaders) will be gathered against Israel. This verse is again a parallel to the scene in Gibeah, in which the tribes assembled against Benjamin (Judg. 20:1-48).

In verse 11, Hosea pictures the tragedy of Ephraim's down-fall into captivity. To understand fully the analogy of the trained heifer, one must know that according to the Mosaic law a threshing heifer was allowed to eat at will while treading out the corn (Deut. 25:4). When Ephraim exchanged the Lord for Baal, she gave up her right to live peaceably in the land. The harness that is to be affixed to them, symbolic of the Assyrian exile, speaks of the harsher tasks of plowing and harrowing. The law of the harvest is again verified.

As the revelations of the utter terror of judgment draw to a close, Hosea reminds his people, "It is time to seek the LORD" (v. 12). Until that final moment when judgment comes crashing down, repentance will reverse the law of the harvest. Sowing righteousness, reaping kindness (God's covenant love [Hebrew, *chesed*]), and breaking up the fallow ground so cluttered with idolatry are three indications of a true heart repentance (cf. Mic. 6:8). The promise in the last line of verse 12 is a glimpse of the glory that is associated with the second coming of Christ. The concept that Christ will rain (Hebrew, *yarah*; literally, "teach") righteousness is a familiar messianic Kingdom blessing (Isa. 2:3; Ezek. 44:23; Mic. 4:2).

In returning to the subject of judgment in verse 13, Hosea reminds Ephraim that she has plowed wickedness instead of righteousness and that she has reaped injustice rather than kindness. Ephraim's steady diet of *lies* would bring the people utter ruin. By trusting in their own way, the people of Israel cut themselves off from the true freedom that is to be found within the will of the Lord. In depending on their numerous warriors (Hebrew, *robh gibborim*; literally, "multitude of mighty men"), the people of Ephraim had gone far afield of the original sentiment expressed by David, "Some boast in chariots, and some in horses; but we will boast in the name of the LORD, our God" (Psalm 20:7).

The devastation of judgment is once again visited in the terrifying scene depicted in verses 14-15. The inhuman carnage inflicted by Shalman (an abbreviated form of Shalmanezer) upon Beth-arbel would soon be brought upon the entire nation. Terror awaits!

5

GOD'S LOVE RESTORES ISRAEL

C. GOD'S LOVE RESTORES A REPENTANT ISRAEL (11:1–14:9)

When Moses first went to Pharaoh to tell him that the Lord said, "Let My people go," Pharaoh responded, "Who is the LORD that I should obey His voice to let Israel go? I do not know the LORD, and besides, I will not let Israel go." (See Exod. 5:1-2.) If Pharaoh could have read this precious book of Hosea, he would have known that the Lord was a *sovereign* God (chaps. 1-3), a *holy* God (chaps. 4-7), a *just* God (chaps. 8-10), and a *loving* God (chaps. 11-14). Pharaoh never received the depth of the knowledge of God that the children of Israel were given through the mouth of the prophet Hosea, and yet the people who heard his words of love and grace were as stony-hearted toward God as was Pharaoh centuries before.

Chapters 11-14 tackle the very issue of Israel's chronic faithlessness and bring to a climax God's sovereign plan for the final redemption of His chosen people (cf. 3:5). The triumph of love presents no conflict to the character of a holy and just God, for in His sovereignty everything that befell Israel was intended to instruct her and bring her back to God (see comment on 7:12).

1. *The compassion of Israel's divine Father* (11:1-11)

Although faced with constant rebellion against His love, the Lord remains steadfast in finding a way to secure redemption for His people. In order to illustrate this relentless love, Hosea delves into the past, present, and future history of redemption. The Lord's self-disclosure in these illustrations is so intense and powerful that it has prompted many to rank this chapter as one of the greatest in the Bible.

a. The past: the love of the Father met by ingratitude (11:

1-4). The eleventh chapter begins with another brief probe into Israel's past to discover the defects in Israel's response to God's love that had led her into apostasy (cf. 9:10, 15; 10:1, 9, 11). Hosea declares in the first verse that *love* (manifested in the redemption from Egypt) was the true basis for Israel's election. The verb *called* (Hebrew, *kara*), meaning "to summon into a relation," speaks of the adoption that has been effected by the Lord for Israel. But the phrase "And out of Egypt I called My son" speaks not only of His love in adopting Israel as His own son, it also foretells the act of love in the distant future when the Lord would call His own Son out of Egypt (Matt. 2: 15). On the significance of Matthew's quotation of this verse, Keil has stated: "Just as Israel grew into a nation in Egypt where it was out of reach of the Canaanitish ways, so was the child Jesus hidden in Egypt from the hostility of Herod."[1]

In response to the love of God as seen in the redemption from Egypt, Israel turned a deaf ear to God's prophets, choosing rather to sacrifice to Baal and burn incense to idols (v. 2; cf. v. 7; 2 Kings 17:13; Jer. 7:25; 25:4; Zech. 1:4). Historically, we can perceive that this is the move from the youth of Israel in her wilderness dependence upon God to her maturity in the land of Canaan (cf. Ezek. 16:1-34). How many times do we rely upon God in our weakness and then neglect Him when He has strengthened and blessed us?

Israel's ingratitude to God becomes even more striking in light of verse 3, in which the prophet records how tenderly and compassionately the Lord taught and cared for His son, Israel. Note how the words of this verse parallel Moses' statement regarding Israel's being carried through the wilderness as a father carries his son (Deut. 1:31-32; 32:10-11). The Lord had led Israel through that wilderness "with cords of a man, with bonds of love" (v. 4), which pictures again the child who is weak on his feet being led gently by his father.

This picture of the Lord's compassion for Israel in her past is completed in the last part of verse 4 by a metaphor that compares the Lord's love for Israel to the farmer who is kind enough to adjust the yoke away from his oxen's jaws when feeding the

---

1. C. F. Keil and F. Delitzsch, *Commentary on the Old Testament in Ten Volumes*, trans. James Martin (Grand Rapids: Eerdmans, n.d.), 10:137.

animal. Truly, God had shown Israel every possible kindness
in the wilderness (Exod. 15:23-25; 16:13-18; 17:6; 40:34; Num.
11:31-32).

b. The present: The ingratitude of Israel met by punishment
(11:5-7). The Israel of Hosea's day is warned in verses 5-7 that
the fatherly care exhibited to them in the past could not be
counted on in the present because of the people's obstinate disobedience to the Lord. Bondage would again come to them, but
a bondage that would be far more severe than had been experienced in Egypt. Israel, by rejection of her divine King and
benevolent Father, had chosen the kingship of Assyria, a cruel
and malevolent tyrant (v. 5). The death and destruction that
will accompany that exchange of kings is represented by a
whirling sword dancing through the city streets (v. 6). Means
of security, typified by the gate bars (Hebrew, *baddim*; literally, "cross beams"), will crumble in the face of the whirling
sword of Assyria.

Do the people repent in the face of such an ominous prediction? The Lord answers this in His lament in verse 7, "So My
people are bent on turning from Me." The frustration experienced by the Lord and His true prophets in attempting to call
Israel back may be summed up in that word *bent* (Hebrew,
tala'), which means "impaled, addicted to, hung." Truly, the
nation was impaled on the hook of sin, and none was willing
to exalt the Lord.

c. The future: The compassion of the Father brings restoration (11:8-11). Verses 8-11 condense the central message of the
entire book—the expression of God's unmerited love toward His
covenant people. God's holiness and justice have exposed a
nation that is as deserving of annihilation as were the wicked
cities of Admah and Zeboiim, which had been consumed along
with Sodom and Gomorrah in a display of God's righteous anger
(Gen. 14:2; 19:27-29; Deut. 29:23). However, the prospect
of annihilating Israel provokes the heart of the Almighty to be
"turned over" within Himself (cf. Jer. 31:20). In the question
"How can I give you up, O Ephraim?" we see that the undying
love of the Father forbids Him from giving up or surrendering
the son He has loved and trained (cf. 11:1-4).

The solution to this great difficulty is presented in verses 9-11.
In stating, "I will not execute My fierce anger," God acknowl-

edges that His covenant love will transcend the legal regulations of the law, which would have dictated that He have His
rebellious son stoned to death (Deut. 21:18-21). The basis for
such forgiveness is simply that He is "God and not man." As
"the Holy One in your midst" God Himself takes the place of
Israel's righteous people, thus guaranteeing that the nation will
be secure (Num. 14:14; Josh. 3:10; Isa. 12:6).[2] Isaiah 63:9 says,
"In all their affliction He was afflicted." The God of Israel is not
some distant clockmaker, who set the world in motion and then
retreated to heaven. On the contrary, He is the same God who
would in His redeeming love send His only Son to stand in the
place of sinners (Rom. 6:23).

With the penalty for sin satisfied in the death of Christ, the
Lord will create in His people a new heart (Jer. 31:33; Ezek. 36:
25-27). With a new heart implanted, Israel will at last "walk
after the LORD" (v. 10). The Lord will call them back to the
land with the roar of a lion. Whereas the metaphor of God as a
lion (Hebrew, *shakal*) is utilized in Hosea 5:14 and 13:7, a
different word for lion (Hebrew, *aryeh*) is employed here in
11:10 to connote the Lord's strength in leading and defending
His people (cf. Jer. 25:30; Joel 3:16; Amos 1:2; 3:8). The
Lord's call to His people will cause them to come trembling in
eagerness "from the west." The direction from which they will
come is significant because a return from an Assyrian or Babylonian exile would be from the *east*. A return from the *west*,
possible only after the dispersion of the Jews in Roman times,
would suggest that this is a reference to the universal regather-
ing of the Jews in the end times (Deut. 30:3-4; Ezek. 20:37-38;
37:1-14). With the knowledge of the Lord in their hearts,
the children of Israel will be settled in the land forever, a promise sealed by the words of verse 11, "declares the LORD" (cf. 2:
21-23).

2. *The longsuffering of Israel's divine Father* (11:12—12:14)

a. Ephraim's unrepentant deceit (11:12—12:1). The glory
of that future day seems distant as Hosea returns to the contemporary reality in verse 12. (In the Hebrew Bible, 11:12 is
the first verse of chapter 12.) Ephraim is charged once again

2. James Luther Mays, *Hosea* (Philadelphia: Westminster, 1969),
p. 158.

with falsehood and deceit (cf. 4:2; 6:7; 7:1, 3, 13; 9:2; 10:4, 13), traits that were also eating away at Judah's faithfulness to God.

The precarious nature of Ephraim's foreign policy is exposed in the first verse of chapter 12. In avowing that "Ephraim feeds on wind," Hosea charges them with maintaining a dangerously futile and elusive foreign policy. The risk of Israel's deceptive diplomacy is likened by Hosea to pursuing the east wind, a reference to the dry, searing sirocco winds that blow from the eastern deserts across Palestine's coastal regions. Assyria, like the blast from the sirocco, is not Ephraim's friend, but an uncontrollable power that will mercilessly consume all that stands before its fiery rage. Whereas it was hazardous to make a covenant with the east wind (2 Kings 17:3), an even greater danger was created when that covenant was broken (2 Kings 17:4-6). Ephraim had deceived the wicked sirocco, a deception that would spell disaster as the enraged east wind swept over the land.

b. Ephraim's precedent for repentance: The example of Jacob (12:2-6). Hosea interrupts his denunciation of Ephraim's deceitfulness with a suggestion that she follow the example of an ancient deceiver, who through repentance obtained the power of God. From the womb until the point that he prevailed in wrestling with the angel, Jacob lived up to the meaning of his name—"supplanter" (Hebrew, *ya-aqob*; literally, "follow at the heel"). Grabbing the heel of his brother (v. 3) prophetically pictured both the gaining of his brother's birthright (Gen. 25:27-34) and the stealing of His father's blessing (Gen. 27:5-29). However, a change occurred in Jacob at the ford of the Jabbok River, where he contended with God and prevailed (Gen. 32:28). Because he had power with God, Jacob's name was changed to Israel (Hebrew, *yisrael*; from the verb *sara,* "to strive," and *el,* "God"). Jacob had always striven for God's blessing through his own deceitful means, but now God would teach Israel and lead him into His way. The patriarch, under his new name, Israel, sought the Lord at Bethel (Gen. 28:11-19; 35:1), the very site where his descendants would worship golden calves (see comment on 10:5). In reminding his contemporaries that when God spoke to Jacob He spoke to all the future generations in Jacob's loins (cf. Heb. 7:9-10), Hosea set the stage for the proclamation of the Lord's name in verse 5.

Ephraim has not rejected a deity made of wood or stone, she has apostatized from the covenant-keeping, self-existent LORD (Hebrew, *YHWH*; derived from the verb *hayah*, "to be"). To the descendants of Israel, God solemnly entrusted His memorial name (Psalm 135:13; cf. Exod. 3:14; 6:3), the praise of which was never to be given to another (Isa. 42:8). At Bethel, Israel the patriarch repented and followed the Lord's instruction to "observe kindness [Hebrew, *chesed*] and justice, and wait for your God continually" (v. 6). On his deathbed, Israel was able still to give this testimony, "For Thy salvation I wait, O LORD" (Gen. 49:18). The plea to Ephraim is that she too will wait upon the Lord and refrain from relying continually on her deceitful dealings with other nations.

c. Ephraim's misplaced love (12:7-14). When the children of Israel entered the promised land, they were specifically told to separate themselves from the practices of the Canaanites, the people whom they were to destroy (Exod. 33:2; Deut. 7:1; 20:17; Josh. 3:10; 17:18). Rebelling against God's plan, the Israelites chose to imbibe the spirit of the Canaanites (Josh. 16:10; 17:12; Judg. 1:29-33). Accordingly, Hosea in verse 7 labels Ephraim "a merchant" (Hebrew, *canaan*), a term that referred to the Canaanites, who were known throughout the world as a merchant people (Isa. 23:11; Ezek. 17:4). Like her Canaanite mentors, Ephraim gained great wealth through employing corrupt business practices such as false balances (Amos 8:5-6). The description of Ephraim's sense of well-being in verse 8 best fits the period of Jeroboam II, a time when power and wealth combined to give the nation its only era of stability and international prestige.

When prosperity finally arrived, Ephraim took it as an indication that nothing was amiss in her relationship to God (Zech. 11:5; cf. Rev. 3:17).[3] Unfortunately, monetary success has never been an accurate barometer of one's status before God (Psalm 37:16; Prov. 11:4; 23:4; Eccles. 8:11-14; Matt. 5:45), something that should be kept in mind today by those Christians who have achieved "the blessings of God" through the same ruthless business ethics used by their unbelieving fellow merchants.

3. Robert Jamieson, A. R. Fausset, and David Brown, *A Commentary, Critical and Explanatory, on the Old and New Testaments* (Grand Rapids: Eerdmans, n.d.), 2:501.

No area of life can be kept hidden from the judgment of God, and thus the Lord in verse 9 says in effect, "Who are you fooling?" Could Israel have forgotten that the "land flowing with milk and honey" (Exod. 3:8) had been a gift of God? Because the Israelites did not acknowledge the giver of their blessings, God would send them back into tents again. The word *tents* (Hebrew, *ohel*) stresses the inconvenience, the unsettledness, and the anxiety of living in a land that is not their own.[4] The "appointed festival" is a reference to the Feast of Tabernacles, the time when Israel was supposed to remember her wilderness wanderings by living in booths (Lev. 23:42).

The announcement of captivity should come as no surprise to a people who had resolutely misplaced their love. God had done more than His part. He not only gave Israel His love, He revealed Himself by means of direct oral instruction through the prophets (e.g., 10:11; Amos 2:6); by numbers of visions (e.g., Amos 7:1–9:15); and by parables (e.g., 2:2-20). Yet, with the divine Word ringing in the people's ears, iniquity and idolatry permeated the land of Israel (vv. 10-11).

In verses 12-14 Hosea once again contrasts the patriarch Jacob with the people of Israel in the prophet's day. Jacob, whose deception of his father had forced him to flee to Padan-aram for safety (Gen. 27:43–28:2), never forsook the Lord he loved even though he had to work almost as a slave (tending sheep) for fourteen years. The nation of Israel, which had been in slavery in Egypt, did not work for her freedom nor for the gracious gift of the promised land (Exod. 3:8-10). Although Israel received every possible benefit from the prophet (Moses) whom God had sent her, she still continued to reject the Lord (Exod. 32:7-14; Num. 14:1-45; 16:30-33).

The Lord's anger, provoked by centuries of ingratitude for His benefits, will result in Israel's being held responsible for her "blood guilt" (v. 14). Blood guilt (Hebrew, *damim*; literally, "bloods") could be incurred through the commission of a number of sins: robbery, bloodshed, adultery, oppression of the poor, dishonesty, idolatry, and the taking of excessive interest (Ezek. 18:10-13). Unless there was a proper atonement for the sin (Deut. 21:7-9), justice against that person had to be exe-

4. Theodore Laetsch, *The Minor Prophets* (St. Louis: Concordia, 1956), p. 98.

cuted or else God would step in to avenge the wronged party (Gen. 4:10-12; 2 Sam. 4:11; Isa. 26:21; Ezek. 24:8).

Throughout the book of Hosea, the word translated *Lord* (LORD in NASB) refers to *YHWH* (see comment on 12:5), the covenant-keeping God of redemption (Exod. 3:14). The one exception to this rule occurs quite significantly in the phrase "So the Lord will leave his bloodguilt on him." Through her persistent sinning, Ephraim had rejected the LORD as her redeemer in favor of the *Lord* (Hebrew, *adonai*; literally, "my master") as her avenger (cf. Gen. 18:27; Judg. 13:8; Ezra 10:3). The word *adonai* is used frequently in the book of Amos, which usage is consistent with the harsher message of that prophecy (Amos 1:8; 3:7, 8, 11, 13; 4:2, 5; 5:3, 16; 7:1, 2, 4, 5, 6, 7, 8; 8:1, 3, 9, 11; 9:1, 5, 8).

3. *Ephraim's tragic response to God's love* (13:1-16)

Knowing that life is filled with choices, one must, as Jacob of old, wait upon the Lord (Gen. 49:18; cf. Psalm 27:14; 40:1; 130:5). Jacob's descendants likewise had to make choices, but in each situation they chose to go against God and His love.

a. Choosing dissipation rather than exaltation (13:1-3). When Joseph brought his two sons to be blessed by Jacob, God prompted the patriarch to exalt Ephraim above the elder son, Manasseh (Gen. 48:18-20). Ephraim's exaltation in Israel was apparent in various phases of the nation's early history (Judg. 8:1-3), but Ephraim's true power was not felt until an Ephraimite named Jeroboam led the revolt against Rehoboam and split the kingdom (1 Kings 11:26—12:28). This same Ephraimite simultaneously introduced calf worship, a wrong that sealed the nation's death warrant (v. 1). In Israelitish thought, Hosea is correct in stating that Ephraim died, because a person who had a deathly illness, was imprisoned or oppressed by an enemy was considered to have already been overcome by the power of death.[5]

Fully devoted to the realm of death, the people are capable of performing such absurdities as kissing (paying homage to) the golden calves (v. 2; cf. 1 Kings 19:18). Having cut themselves off from the Lord and His righteousness, Israel's sin increased

---

5. Hans Walter Wolff, *Hosea*, trans. Gary Stansell, ed. Paul D. Hanson (Philadelphia: Fortress, 1974), p. 225.

like an unchecked infection. The inevitable result of that infectious increase in sin was the complete dissipation of the nation, pictured in verse 3 by the morning cloud, the dew, the chaff, and the smoke out of a chimney (cf. 6:4; Psalm 1:4).

b. Choosing destruction rather than salvation (13:4-8). Whereas an understanding of the knowledge of God would have permitted Israel to make the right choices, she forgot that the Lord was her Savior and followed after destruction (cf. comment on 4:1). As an example of that forgetfulness, the first commandment is referred to in verse 4 (Exod. 20:3-6; cf. Isa. 43:11; 45:21-22). Even though it had been taught so extensively to the people, the first commandment was lost in Hosea's day under a refuse heap of graven images. Although the people of Israel ignored God's commandments, they were not averse to fattening themselves with all the benefits of being in God's pasture (cf. 4:16; Deut. 8:2-4). Having stuffed themselves with many a "Thanksgiving dinner," the Israelites, like many Americans today, forgot that the thanks belonged to God and not themselves (vv. 5-6; Deut. 32:15).

Paralleling the sequence established in verses 1-3, Hosea once again follows his announcement of the sin with a revelation of its consequences (vv. 7-8). The judgment (destruction) is the same as that promised by Moses centuries earlier (Deut. 8:11-20). God's power in executing this judgment is likened to that of five wild animals: the strength of a lion, the cunning of a leopard, the wild fury of a mother bear robbed of her cubs, the eagerness of a lioness, and the ferocity of a wild beast. From this scene of carnage, one poignant expression especially catches the horror of the judgment: "And I will tear open their chests." This phrase, which speaks literally of baring the very enclosure of the heart, alludes to the fact that Israel would be helplessly exposed to all who would attack her.

c. Choosing a human king rather than the King of kings (13: 9-11). As Israel plunges headlong over the waterfall, the Lord laments that His people have done everything possible to navigate around His helping hand. To illustrate, the Lord cites the rejection of His kingship over the nation. Prompted by a desire to be like other nations, Israel asked God for a human king, a request that God in His righteous anger granted (v. 11*a*; 1 Sam. 8:5-22). Saul, the man chosen to replace God as king, soon rebelled against the Lord and was removed (v. 11*b*; 1 Sam. 15: 22-23). The Lord permitted Jeroboam I to take the rulership of the ten tribes, promising security if he would walk in the way of the Lord as David had done (1 Kings 11:38). Jeroboam did not live up to this condition, rather, he and all his successors followed in the way of Saul (2 Kings 17:18-23).

d. Choosing death rather than life (13:12-16). In the closing verses of this thirteenth chapter, the Lord again challenges the chosen people to seek His compassion and live. Like the previous sections of this chapter, Ephraim's sin is first considered. Verse 12 asserts that Ephraim's iniquity (Hebrew, *awon*; literally, "perversity") is bound up (Hebrew, *tsarur*), or more literally "filled to overflowing."[6] With the weight of this iniquity demanding retribution, Ephraim's sin is stored up (Hebrew, *tsepunah*; literally, "hidden, treasured up") by the Lord for that great Judgment Day (cf. Rev. 20:12-13).[7]

The Lord digresses from the scene of judgment and in verses 13-14 reminds Israel that restoration, not retribution, is the goal of His sovereign plan for Israel. By the familiar figure of a woman in travail (cf. Isa. 13:8; Jer. 4:31; 49:24; Mic. 4:9-10; Matt. 24:8; Rev. 12:2), Hosea alerts Israel to the reality that the sufferings and calamities (each "pains of childbirth") represent God's refining judgments, which will lead Israel to a complete transformation—a new birth.[8] The prospect of this birth is foiled by Ephraim (the unborn son), who refuses to be liberated by the pulsating birth pangs, and thus causes the womb to become his grave (v. 13).

Like a ray of sunlight penetrating through a sky filled with storm clouds, the fourteenth verse bursts upon this dark scene with the light of the good news. For a generation that was soon to walk literally into the valley of the shadow of death, this verse offers afresh the promise of God to redeem Israel from that realm of death into which she was falling. How will the Lord ransom Israel from sheol and redeem her from death? The answer is to be found in the death and resurrection of the sin-

6. A link between verses 12 and 13 is to be found in the word *tsarur*, a form of which is used in Jeremiah 4:31 and 49:24 to describe the agony of travail in childbirth. Thus, Ephraim's iniquity initiated the agony that eventually led to her death.
7. Laetsch, p. 103.
8. Keil, 10:159.

less Son of God (Acts 4:12; 15:11; Rom. 5:9; 6:23; 10:9-10; Heb. 9:22). Christ's overpowering of death and hades (the Greek equivalent of sheol, rendered "death" in 1 Cor. 15:55) prompted the apostle Paul to quote this verse in his teaching on the resurrection (1 Cor. 15:55-56).

The great revelations of the fourteenth verse are concluded with the phrase "Compassion will he hid from My sight." "Compassion" (Hebrew, *nocham*) is a translation of the verb *nacham*, which means "repentance." In Scripture, the word *nacham* is frequently utilized to state that the Lord had (speaking from a human standpoint) changed His mind (Gen. 6:6-7; Exod. 32:12, 14; Judg. 2:18; 1 Sam. 15:11, 35; 2 Sam. 24:16; 1 Chron. 21:15; Jer. 18:8, 10; Amos 7:3, 6; Jonah 3:9-10). To say that God "repents" of a plan is merely a convenience for finite man to understand the process involved in God's sovereign plan (1 Sam. 15:29; Psalm 110:4; Zech. 8:14-15; cf. James 1:17). One commentator has noted that the Lord's statement that He will not repent may include both a reference to the certainty of judgment for Ephraim as well as the assurance of redemption from death and sheol.[9]

The nature of Ephraim's judgment again occupies Hosea's thoughts as he continues his prophecy in verses 15-16. (Verse 16 in the Hebrew Bible is the first verse of chapter 14.) Hosea speaks again of Israel's two-faced foreign policy and warns that although Israel is flourishing "among the reeds" (a reference to Egypt), the "east wind" (Assyria, see comment on 12:1) will sweep down upon the land and cause it to become dry and barren. This judgment upon Israel is justified because of the rebellion that separated her from the love of God. A brutish bloodbath is the recompense for such rebellion (cf. 10:13-14; 2 Kings 15:16; Isa. 13:16; Amos 1:13).

4. *The final triumph of God's grace* (14:1-9)

The sovereignty, holiness, justice, and love of God have all worked in unison to achieve the final triumph of God's grace. Just as Hosea personally effected the redemption of his wife (3:1-3), so also the Lord in this fourteenth chapter concludes the redemption that will restore His wife, Israel.

a. The final call receives a repentant response (14:1-3). As

9. Homer Hailey, *A Commentary on the Minor Prophets* (Grand Rapids: Baker, 1972), p. 182.

Hosea reached the close of his prophetic ministry, his lips never tired of forming that one word *return* (Hebrew, *shub*). The thrust of his ministry centered on his desire for the people to return to the God of covenant love, a response that his backslidden countrymen would not make. Yet, in these final verses, the curtain is drawn aside, and Hosea is permitted to hear that final *shub* that will awaken in Israel a full repentance (v. 1). As the second verse underscores, the nature of this repentance must include a confession of sin and a request for God's grace.

Knowing that Israel had mechanically offered sacrifices without thinking of their meaning (cf. 6:6; 1 Sam. 15:22; Jer. 7:23; Matt. 9:13; 12:7), the prophet asks that the repentant ones present the fruit, or more literally the "calves," of their lips. In other words, the calves the Lord wants sacrificed should take the form of prayer for forgiveness (Psalm 51:17) and praise for God's grace (Psalm 69:30-31; 71:23-24; Heb. 13:15).

These *words* of repentance (v. 2) are backed up by the *actions* of verse 3, a verification of the teaching principle that something is not truly learned until it results in a changed behavior. In this third verse, Israel repents specifically of three besetting sins: reliance upon Assyria for salvation, dependence upon Egypt for military aid, and trust in man-made idols for spiritual blessing. Each of those sins drives home the extent to which Israel had rebelled against God in searching for security and blessing (7:11; 8:6; 13:2). Israel's repentance from her rebellion is especially typified in the phrase "We will not ride on horses." By this statement Israel was finally admitting that the importation of horses from Egypt (begun in the time of Solomon, 1 Kings 10:28) was in direct rebellion to the command of Moses not to return to Egypt in search of horses (Deut. 17:16). To the Hebrews, the horse represented a weapon of war, the multiplication of which signalled a lack of trust in the Lord (cf. Psalm 20:7; 33:17; Prov. 21:31; Isa. 30:16; 31:1; Amos 4:10).

In the final line of this third verse, "For in Thee the orphan finds mercy," Israel at last realizes that she has been running from her only true friend. The allusion to the plight of the orphan is appropriate, because the Scriptures are replete with references to the undying mercy of God for the orphan (Deut. 14:29; 16:11; 24:17-21; 26:12-13; 27:19; Psalm 10:14; 146:9; Isa.

10:2; Jer. 5:28; 7:6; 22:3; Zech. 7:10; Mal. 3:5).[10]

b. Repentance brings full restoration (14:4-5*a*). God's love stands ready to restore the repentant sinner today in the same miraculous way that it will restore Israel in that great future day when the nation returns to the Lord (Rom. 11:26-27).

Verses 4-7 detail the restoration of Israel from two vantage points: the work of the Lord in restoration ("I will") and the result of that work in the people ("He will"). For God's part (vv. 4-5*a*), restoration will involve three elements: (1) a healing of the apostasy that had separated the nation from God (cf. Exod. 15:26); (2) a gracious gift of love that freely forgives all sin (cf. Rom. 3:24); and (3) a renewal of the blessings on the land that will be poured out like the dew. As a symbol that had previously served as a metaphor for the fleeting nature of Israel's loyalty (6:4; 13:3), the dew now becomes an emblem of the refreshing benefits that will fall upon the nation through the blessing of God. Coming upon the nation suddenly in the night, the dew promotes new life on the soil that had been parched by the harsh east wind.[11]

c. The fruits of true repentance (14:5*b*-7). From his own personal tragedy, Hosea knew all too well the bitter fruits of harlotry—both physical and spiritual (see comments on 1:3-9). But in Hosea's family and in the nation of Israel, which the prophet's family symbolized, repentance effected an exchange of those bitter fruits of harlotry for the sweet fruits of repentance (1:10—2:1; 2:21-23; 3:1-5).

In picturing the beauty of the fruit that Israel will cultivate in her new relationships to God (Isa. 62:3; Jer. 32:41; Zeph. 3:16-17; Zech. 9:16-17), Hosea employs much of the imagery that is found in the love song of the Hebrews, the Song of Solomon.[12] The first token by which Hosea describes the change in Israel is the lily (Hebrew, *shoshannah*; the name *Susannah* is derived from this). Emphasizing Israel's newfound beauty

10. For an excellent study on the subject of the orphan in the Bible, consult Richard D. Patterson, "The Widow, the Orphan and the Poor in the Old Testament and the Extra Biblical Literature," *Bibliotheca Sacra* (July-September 1973): 223-34.

11. Page H. Kelley, "The Holy One in the Midst of Israel: Redeeming Love (Hosea 11-14)," *Review and Expositor* 72, no. 4 (Fall 1975): 471.

12. E W. Hengstenberg, *Christology of the Old Testament*, trans. Theod. Meyer and James Martin (Grand Rapids: Kregel, 1956), 1:181.

and purity, the word *lily* is frequently employed by Solomon in his poetic metaphors (Song of Sol. 2:1-2, 16; 4:5; 5:13; 6:2-3; 7:2).

Perhaps because the lily is not emblematic of strength or stability, Hosea immediately draws the attention of his listeners to the image of the firm and deeply rooted cedars of Lebanon. For the people who have suffered the bitter fruit of being without "roots" for countless centuries, the prospect of being firmly planted in the land is a dream that has still not fully come true (2:23; cf. Psalm 1:3; 92:13).

In addition to the lily and the rooted cedar tree, Hosea enumerates three more fruits of repentance in verse 6. First, the firmly rooted nation will begin to display *new life,* the token of which will be the sprouts on the shoots (cf. Gen. 49:22). Ephraim will finally begin to be "fruitful."

In desiring to speak of yet another fruit, *usefulness,* Hosea likens the renewed Israel to the olive tree. The people of Hosea's day placed a high premium on the oil extracted from the olive trees, which was useful not only domestically (1 Kings 17:14; 2 Kings 4:6-7), but also in foreign trade (2:5; 12:1).

The third fruit of repentance mentioned in the sixth verse is the fresh *fragrance* that will characterize Israel. Likened to the smell of a forest of cedars of Lebanon (cf. Song of Sol. 5:15; 7:11), Israel's return to the Lord will mean an end of the stench that emanated from every idol that polluted the land in Hosea's day (e.g., Ezek. 36:18).

Whereas the fruits of repentance noted in verses 5-6 have applied just to Israel, the seventh verse extends the sphere of blessing to include those Gentiles who come to Israel for blessing (Isa. 2:4; 16:1-5; 18:1-7; 19:16-25; 45:14; Zech. 8:20-23; 14: 16-19).[13] Israel, which should have been a blessing to her neighbors from the time she first entered the land, will at last fulfill the destiny for which God chose her (Exod. 19:5-6). When

13. A question in interpretation confronts the reader in verse 7. Do the words "Those who live in his shadow" refer to the shadow of the Lord or the shadow of Israel? An examination of the passages that speak of the shadow of the Lord (Psalm 17:8; 91:1; Isaiah 51:16) do not reveal any application to the image of a tree's giving shade. Accordingly, the heavier argument can be adduced for the view that would see this as the nation of Israel. The context supplies the major weight for this interpretation, because the word "his" applies only to Israel in verses 5-6.

the nations do look to Israel for their salvation, "they will blossom like the vine" (cf. Song of Sol. 2:13; 6:11; 7:12). Truly the world united under the Messiah reigning from Israel will witness the establishment of a high quality of life that is not equalled today.

One final fruit of repentance that will benefit both Israel and the nations is expressed in the words "His renown will be like the wine of Lebanon" (v. 7; cf. Song of Sol. 1:2, 4; 4:10). The wine of Lebanon was celebrated in Hosea's day for its aroma, flavor, and medicinal restorative properties.[14] This metaphor would certainly accord with the scriptural evidence that the Millennium will be a time when the Messiah ruling from Israel will bring healing to the entire world (Mic. 4:6-7; Zeph. 3:19; cf. Isa. 29:17-19; 33:24; 35:3-6; Jer. 30:17; 31:8; Ezek. 34:16).

d. Israel eternally betrothed to God (14:8). In the second chapter, the Lord announced that He would betroth Himself to Israel forever (2:18-20). The interlude of disciplinary chastisement between chapters 2 and 14, proved necessary by Israel's chronic faithlessness (see comment on 6:4), is finally brought to a close as Israel in this verse is eternally betrothed to God. The statements made in verse 8 resemble marriage vows, with Ephraim speaking lines one and three, and the Lord responding in lines two and four.[15]

With verses 5-7 speaking of the new life that has been created in Ephraim, one would expect an Ephraim that had been joined to idols (4:17) to say, "What more have I to do with idols?" In response to Ephraim's declaration, the Lord promises to hear and protect His wife. Israel, reflecting on the metaphors that have linked her new creation to various forms of luxuriant plant

14. Jamieson, Fausset and Brown, 2:508.
15. Supporting the view that this is a dialogue between Ephraim and God are Charles F. Pfeiffer, "Hosea," in *The Wycliffe Bible Commentary,* ed. Charles F. Pfeiffer and Everett F. Harrison (Chicago: Moody, 1962), p. 817 and Clyde T. Francisco, "Expository Outline of the Book of Hosea," *Review and Expositor,* 72:4 (Fall 1975) 493. However, neither the *New American Standard Bible* (NASB) nor the King James Version (KJV) may be adduced to support this view. The NASB regards the Lord as speaking to Ephraim in each line of the eighth verse. The word "O" is added by the NASB translators, based on the assumption that Ephraim is a noun of address. On the other hand, the KJV regards the entire verse as a statement of faith from Ephraim to God. The translators of this version have added the words "shall say" after the word "Ephraim" to indicate who is speaking.

life (vv. 5-7), announces, "I am like a luxuriant cypress." The evergreen cypress emphasizes the qualities of permanent freshness and fruitfulness; it stands in contrast to the "old Ephraim," which rotted away for her apostasy (5:12). The last line of the verse, "From Me comes your fruit," is the Lord's final reminder to Ephraim that every blessing has come from above.

e. The final word (14:9). In concluding his comprehensive exposition of the sovereignty (chaps. 1-3), holiness (chaps. 4-7), justice (chaps. 8-10), and love (chaps. 11-14) of God, Hosea appeals to those listening not only to *understand* (Hebrew, *yaben*) intellectually his prophecy, but also to *discern* (Hebrew, *nabon*) how that knowledge can apply to daily living. A constant understanding and application of the prophecy will lead men into the ways of the Lord, a guaranteed certainty because the one who knows the prophecy of Hosea also will know the Lord.

In terms of results, the preaching of Hosea was a failure. His contemporaries did not walk in the paths of the righteous but rather stumbled into captivity. God's standard, however, is not success but *faithfulness* (Num. 12:7; 1 Sam. 2:35; Neh. 9:8; Prov. 11:13; 20:6-7; 28:20; Jer. 23:28), and on that score Hosea was without rival among the Old Testament prophets. By enduring through the profligacy of both his wife and his country, Hosea was used by the Lord in contributing a revelation of God's character. That revelation should motivate us diligently to seek to understand and apply the message of Hosea to our hearts.

BIBLIOGRAPHY

Bennett, T. Miles. *Hosea: Prophet of God's Love*. Grand Rapids: Baker, 1975.

Bright, John. *A History of Israel*. Philadelphia: Westminster, 1959.

Coleman, Shalom. *Hosea Concepts in the Midrash and Talmud*. New York: Block, 1960.

Feinberg, Charles L. *The Minor Prophets*. Chicago: Moody, 1977.

Francisco, Clyde T. "Expository Outline of the Book of Hosea." *Review and Expositor* 72, no. 4 (Fall 1975): 487-93.

Freeman, Hobart E. *An Introduction to the Old Testament Prophets*. Chicago: Moody, 1968.

Freeman, James. *Manners and Customs in the Bible*. Plainfield, N.J.: Logos, 1972.

Garland, D. David. *Hosea*. Grand Rapids: Zondervan, 1975.

Given, J. J. "Hosea." In *The Pulpit Commentary*, edited by H. D. M. Spence and Joseph S. Exell. Vol. 13. Grand Rapids: Eerdmans, 1950.

Hailey, Homer. *A Commentary on the Minor Prophets*. Grand Rapids: Baker, 1972.

Harper, William Rainey. *A Critical and Exegetical Commentary on Amos and Hosea*. In *The International Critical Commentary*. Edited by Samuel Rolles Driver, Alfred Plummer, and Charles Augustus Briggs. Edinburgh: T. & T. Clark, 1905.

Hengstenberg, E. W. *Christology of the Old Testament*. Translated by Theod. Meyer and James Martin. Vol. 1. Grand Rapids: Kregel, 1956.

Jamieson, Robert; Fausset, A. R.; and Brown, David. *A Commentary, Critical and Explanatory, on the Old and New Testaments*. Vol. 2. Grand Rapids: Eerdmans, n.d.

Keil, C. F., and Delitzsch, F. *Commentary on the Old Testament in Ten Volumes*. Translated by James Martin. Vol. 10. Grand Rapids: Eerdmans, n.d.

Kelley, Page H. "The Holy One in the Midst of Israel: Redeeming Love (Hosea 11-14)." *Review and Expositor* 72, no. 4 (Fall 1975): 465-72.

Kittel, Gerhard. *Theological Dictionary of the New Testament*. Translated and edited by Geoffrey W. Bromiley. Vol. 2. Grand Rapids: Eerdmans, 1964.

Laetsch, Theodore. *The Minor Prophets*. St. Louis: Concordia, 1956.

Mays, James Luther. *Hosea*. Philadelphia: Westminster, 1969.

Morgan, G. Campbell. *Hosea: The Heart and Holiness of God*. Grand Rapids: Baker, 1974.

Patterson, Richard D. "The Widow, the Orphan and the Poor in the Old Testament and Extra Biblical Literature." *Bibliotheca Sacra* (July-September 1973): 223-34.

Pfeiffer, Charles F. "Hosea." In *The Wycliffe Bible Commentary*, edited by Charles F. Pfeiffer and Everett F. Harrison. Chicago: Moody, 1962.

Pusey, E. B. *The Minor Prophets: A Commentary*. Vol. 1. Grand Rapids: Baker, 1950.

Rowley, H. H. "The Marriage of Hosea." *Bulletin of the John Rylands Library* 39, no. 1 (September 1956): 200-233.

Scott, Jack B. *The Book of Hosea*. Grand Rapids: Baker, 1971.

Tatford, Frederick. *Prophet of a Broken Home*. Sussex: Prophetic Witness, 1974.

Wolff, Hans Walter. *Hosea*. Translated by Gary Stansell. Edited by Paul D. Hanson. Philadelphia: Fortress, 1974.

Yates, Kyle M. *Preaching from the Prophets*. Nashville: Broadman, 1942.

AMOS

by

GARY G. COHEN

To Gerald Schatz, a true friend

ACKNOWLEDGMENTS

Special thanks is offered to the editors at Moody Press, especially Garry Knussman, for their scholarly and always able work.

6

INTRODUCTION TO AMOS

HISTORICAL BACKGROUND

Amos arrived on the scene of a prosperous nation that was growing in immorality and in indifference toward God and His laws. "Optimism in spite of distant dangers" might have been the headline on the editorial page of the *Walls of Samaria Journal* on the morning when Amos arrived in the capital city of the Northern Kingdom (Israel). The Southern Kingdom (Judah) was also amid a time of general prosperity, and therefore Amos's message was viewed with irritation by the contented, well-to-do crowds from both halves of the Land of Israel.[1] With business barometers up, despite the usual complaining from the poor and the fanatically religious, warnings of coming, divinely sent troubles seemed almost irrelevant. Amos's yelling about the falling morals of the community appeared to be coming from a *Chasid* ("pious holy-person"), one out of tune with modern folkways and mores. His message was mere irrelevant chatter.

Uzziah (767-739 B.C.) reigned in Judah. Jeroboam II (793-753 B.C.) ruled in semi-idolatry over the northern ten tribes, sitting and looking down on his domain from proud Samaria's heights. All seemed calm on the political fronts, except for a periodic threat from the cruel sleeping lion Assyria, almost a thousand miles to the east, beyond the Golan cliffs and the Euphrates River.

In Judah Uzziah began his reign as a righteous king, and the Lord's blessing was upon that land. Second Chronicles 26 says that Uzziah subdued the Philistines to the southwest, that the Ammonites in the west paid him tribute, and also that he con-

---

1. "Land of Israel" is the traditional name for Palestine, encompassing both the northern and southern halves. Significantly, these words in Hebrew, *Eretz Yisroel*, begin the May 14, 1948, Declaration of Independence of the nation of Israel.

quered the Arabians (v. 7). The Arabians (*Arabim* in Hebrew) probably included the Edomites to the south and also
the scattered tribes of the northwestern edge of the Arabian
peninsula. We are even told in 2 Chronicles 26:8 that Uzziah's
fame spread "to the border of Egypt," and from that we may
infer that the Egyptians had heard of his military strength.
Uzziah had a large standing army and had refortified Jerusalem,
measures designed to make Egypt and others think twice before
considering any kind of march against Jerusalem and Judah
(2 Chronicles 26:11-15).

Judah was the land from which Amos came. It was not the
land of his ministry.

In Israel were the people to whom God called Amos to proclaim His message. Here Jeroboam II sat upon a secure throne
and ruled over a stable nation—or so the situation appeared.
Israel was experiencing a new boom of prosperity under that
monarch's strong hand and long reign of forty-one years
(2 Kings 14:23). Despite the evil nature of King Jeroboam II,
God nevertheless chose to have mercy upon the Northern Kingdom during that period of calm before the gathering storm.

Under Jeroboam II the boundary lines of the nation were
strengthened in every direction. In the west the Lebanon
coastal plain was retaken from Syria, while to the north even
Damascus itself was at last subjugated to Israel. At the same
time, to the southeast Jeroboam II became the controlling force
over pagan Moab. To the direct south, Jeroboam II's father
Jehoash (Joash) had previously defeated Judah in war, and
Jeroboam II retained that supremacy in strength over Jerusalem and the Southern Kingdom (2 Kings 14:11-14, 23-28).
Uzziah, in turn, kept Ammon under control to the east, Edom
to the south, and Philistia to the southwest. While his supremacy radiated out in every direction, Jeroboam II's plans did not
include public interference and complaining by some uninvited
prophet from the south.

So, the land upon which Amos was about to unleash his message of final warning was one with ironclad military strength.
Israel at last had arrived at her dream defensive configuration;
she was stronger than her adjacent neighbors in every direction. Not only was Jeroboam II triumphant at last over Syria,
Israel's traditional thorn to the north, but Syria was fully occu-

pied with Assyria because she feared that that lion might someday awaken and devour her. Syria was thus Israel's buffer
against Assyria; and to the south, Judah was Israel's buffer
against Egypt. Then, with the endless Mediterranean Sea to
the west and the seemingly impassable Golani mountains to
the east, the perfect ring had been formed at last.

What could threaten so strong an Israel? Surely not some
backward prophet babbling something about religion, which
only the poorer rabbis would even care about.

Prosperity. That was the big news in Samaria's business centers. The peace, power, and conquest of Jeroboam II over so
extended a duration of time had to have favorable effects on
the merchant trade of the Northern Kingdom. Now a once-
struggling nation of farmers was seeing trade expanding and
new markets opening in every direction. Luxurious furniture
of wood and ivory began to be observed moving in the streets of
Samaria almost daily. Such furniture made its way to the upper
royal palace and to the houses of the noble rich. A growing
wealthy class was becoming noticeable, and citizens of the upper brackets were able to afford both summer and winter residences of fine stone.

New homes were not the half of it. Luxurious food weighed
down elegant tables, and flutes and lyres filled the balmy air
of Samaria with music. For the wealthy at that time it must
have seemed like a bit of heaven, a delightful time to be alive.

Yet a problem seethed below the surface of all this froth.
Jeroboam II was still following the idolatrous religion that was
conceived by his namesake Jeroboam I (931-910 B.C.), a century and a half earlier. Jeroboam I had instituted Bethel and
Dan as dual cities of worship for the Northern tribes. At each
city he had erected a huge ornamented altar upon which a
golden calf stood to be worshiped (1 Kings 12:26-33). Thus
there were two cities of worship in the north, to only one (Jerusalem) in the south; and at each of the two northern worship
cities there stood lifted up a golden calf such as Aaron had cast
to Israel's folly some seven centuries before. To make the situation more complicated, the two calves of the Northern Kingdom
were generally called "god," that is *El* or *Elohim*, rather than
Baal by their devotees. To those who loved the Lord, such a
distinction did little to cover open idolatry and disobedience.

That false religious system still stood out clearly as the chief blot upon the cheerful and secure Northern Kingdom, and a man named Amos was about to stop the party and point this out.

AMOS THE MAN

The name *Amos* comes from the infrequently used Hebrew verb *amas,* "to load a burden upon an animal." Amos is the noun form, meaning "a burden." This word for *burden,* however, is *not* the more frequently used similar word *masa,* which is used countless times throughout the Old Testament, for example in Isaiah 15:1 (KJV). There it says, "The *burden* of Moab" (italics added), that is, God's burdensome message of judgment aimed at Moab.

Whether for some unknown family reason Amos was given this name, or whether it was an epithet thrown at him by those who hated him, we may only speculate. If the latter explanation is the true one, it might well be translated as "the pain." Then it would have been a name of scorn hung upon the lowly prophet by his adversaries. From what we can deduce about his character in this small book of prophecy, Amos seems as though he was just the sort of fellow who would have accepted that label with righteous pride. In so doing he may have taken it as his own and as God's mantle for his mission of rebuke to a nation of lethargic sinners.

In 1:1 he is marked as one who came out of the "sheepherders from Tekoa," and in 7:14 it is added that he also was a "grower of sycamore figs." He further disclaimed in 7:14 that he was neither a professional prophet nor even a son of a prophet. Had the Lord erred in sending a farmer instead of a more esteemed member of the clergy?

We see that God had called an unspoiled and plain man to rebuke a spoiled and fancy-living generation. Amos was a herdsman of sheep, or oxen, or both; and apparently he also raised *shiqmim* (sycamore figs). Such figs were a kind of mulberry figs indigenous to the area and are not to be confused with the sycamore tree found in the Western Hemisphere. The various Bible commentators who are botanically inclined argue endlessly on the exact genus and species of the fruit signified by the ancient Hebrew word. Today we simply do not know such classification for certain, just as we do not know the size of Amos's livestock herds. Some would prefer to picture the prophet living in poverty in a small yard with only a pair of sheep and one fig tree, whereas others would prefer to portray him almost as a "Texas gentleman rancher" with herds grazing on sprawling acres, orchards of figs, and a contingent of helpers at his employ—someone like the late President Lyndon B. Johnson. We simply do not know. The point is, Amos was not a professional prophet tutored in the rabbinical schools of Jerusalem; neither was he a priest. He was rather a shepherd and farmer who lived upon the unspoiled, simple local diet of that area, much the same as John the Baptist lived off honey and wild locusts (Matt. 3:4).

Tekoa, the town from which Amos came, lay five miles southeast of Bethlehem, quite near to Jerusalem, the capital of Judah. Tekoa was one of the cities fortified by Rehoboam, Solomon's son and king of Judah, as an outpost to delay any attack from the south that might encircle Jerusalem (see Jer. 6:1). Besides being the birthplace of one of David's thirty mighty men (2 Sam. 23:26), it was a town of little note among the hills of Judah. This fact further solidifies the image of Amos as the simple man whom God chose to rebuke the arrogant sinners of that age.

The fact that Amos hailed from the Southern Kingdom provided another key reason for his hearers in the Northern Kingdom to disdain him. How easily it would be recognized that this denouncer of the north's royal worship city Bethel came from the environs of Jerusalem, the rival worship city of Judah (7:12-13).

In spite of all Amos's adverse characteristics—simple occupation, simple diet, no formal religious credentials, legally a foreigner to the Northern Kingdom—he was the man whom God called to rebuke Samaria, with her royalty, pomp, and false priestcraft.

It seems like a huge mistake; but God does not make even small mistakes. Amos's God-inspired rebukes, his plain speech, his holy ethics, and his biting rural imagery were precisely the words the Northern Kingdom needed to hear. Unknowingly, she was sleeping on a political time bomb that was about to explode, and Amos's cry in the night was her final chance for awakening and national survival. A nationwide repentance was what was needed to enlist God's forgiveness and then His help to hold back the fierce Assyrians who were already sharpening their knives to the east. God selected, when all is considered, the ideal man for a message of "Repent—or perish!"

OUTLINE

 I. Author and Theme of the Book (1:1-2)

 II. Judgment Against the Heathen Nations (1:3—2:16)
   A. Against Syria (1:3-5)
   B. Against the Philistines (1:6-8)
   C. Against Tyre (1:9-10)
   D. Against Edom (1:11-12)
   E. Against Ammon (1:13-15)
   F. Against Moab (2:1-3)

 III. Judgment Against God's Chosen People (2:4-16)
   A. Against Judah (2:4-5)
   B. Against Israel (2:6-16)
     1. Israel's waywardness (2:6-8)
     2. God's past blessings on Israel (2:9-11)
     3. Israel's perfidy (2:12-13)
     4. Israel's judgment certain (2:14-16)

 IV. Amos's Sermons Against Israel (3:1—6:14)
   A. Judgment announced against Israel (3:1-8)
     1. The betrothal of Israel to God (3:1-2)
     2. The bisection of Israel from God (3:3)
     3. The prophet's bemoaning of the separation (3:4-8)
   B. Samaria's coming doom (3:9-15)
     1. The prophet summons the enemies (3:9)
     2. The belligerence of the people of Samaria (3:10)
     3. The banishment of Samaria and Israel (3:11-15)
   C. Samaria's failure to heed God's chastenings (4:1-13)
     1. Your cows will collapse (4:1-3)
     2. Your ceremonies will cease (4:4-5)
     3. Your chastisement has called (4:6-11)
     4. Your Creator is coming (4:12-13)

D. Samaria's false religion condemned (5:1-27)
   1. God's dirge for Israel (5:1-3)
   2. God's directions to Israel (5:4-7)
   3. God's deity over Israel (5:8-9)
   4. God's dismay over Israel (5:10-13)
   5. God's demands for Israel (5:14-15)
   6. God's drawing near to Israel (5:16-20)
   7. God's denial of Israel (5:21-26)
   8. God's decision for Israel (5:27)
E. Samaria's ease to be turned to suffering (6:1-14)
   1. God's message to those at ease in Zion—calamity coming (6:1-3)
   2. God's message to those in luxury in Samaria—exile coming (6:4-7)
   3. God's message to those in arrogance—lowliness coming (6:8-11)
   4. God's message to those confident in Israel—affliction coming (6:12-14)

V. Amos's Visions of Coming Judgment (7:1—9:15)
   A. Vision of the locust swarm (7:1-3)
   B. Vision of the fire (7:4-6)
   C. Vision of the plumb line (7:7-9)
   D. Historical interlude: opposition at Bethel (7:10-17)
      1. Amaziah's report (7:10-11)
      2. Amaziah's rebuke (7:12-13)
      3. Amos's reply (7:14-15)
      4. Amaziah's reward (7:16-17)
   E. Vision of the summer fruit (8:1-14)
      1. The sinful condition of Israel (8:1-6)
         a. Ripe fruit (8:1-3)
         b. Ripe nation (8:4-6)
      2. The suffering coming to Israel (8:7-14)
         a. Sackcloth for dress (8:7-10)
         b. Famine from God's Word (8:11-14)
   F. Vision of the Lord beside the altar (9:1-10)
      1. The present destruction of the sinful kingdom (9:1-6)
         a. The holy pursuit (9:1-4)
         b. The holy Person (9:5-6)

   2. The future restoration of the righteous kingdom
      (9:7-15)
      a. The sinful in Israel removed (9:7-8*a*)
      b. The remnant out of Israel retained (9:8*b*-10)
      c. The house of David repaired (9:11-12)
      d. The people and land of Israel restored (9:13-15)

7

NATIONS ARE JUDGED BY GOD

I. AUTHOR AND THEME OF THE BOOK (1:1-2)

"How long will judgment tarry?" is one of the basic questions of life. The psalmist cries, "How long. . . . Pour out Thy wrath upon the nations. . . . For they have devoured Jacob, and laid waste his habitation" (Psalm 79:5-7). There have been times, such as when the Israelites wandered in the wilderness and carried the Ark with them daily, that God's judgment struck almost instantaneously after a sin (e.g., Num. 16:1-35). This is not, however, God's ordinary way of governing His world. Judgment upon the wicked is often delayed in order to give an opportunity for repentance (2 Pet. 3:9) and in order to let the situation develop so that the wickedness will be openly exposed as fully deserving judgment (e.g., Gen. 15:16). Eventually judgment always comes. It has been said, "The wheels of God's justice grind slowly, but when they come they do grind finely." This is the basic message of the first three chapters of Amos.

That the Lord selected a sheepherder from quiet Tekoa, ten miles southeast of Jerusalem, to announce His cataclysmic judgments is one of God's sovereign ironies. Perhaps God, in that situation, did not want His prophet to be a wise intellectual who might debate with the learned royal sinners in the palace of Samaria. God preferred His spokesman to announce His visions as irrevocable fait accompli, and such a one as Amos from Tekoa would lend an aura of undeniable finality to the visions. However, Tekoa also may have been a center of godly wisdom (see 2 Sam. 14:2, 4, 9).

"Two years before the earthquake" (v. 1). This quake must have been a fearful and memorable one, long talked about in that region. Two and a half centuries later the prophet Zechariah says the flight that will occur at the Messiah's second coming will be "as you fled before the earthquake in the days of

Uzziah king of Judah" (Zech. 14:5). We can place Uzziah's reign at 767-739 B.C., but we have no data that might help us precisely to place the quake within his reign.[1]

The proclamation at the beginning of the prophecy that Amos saw his vision "two years before the earthquake" seems to have a signfiicance beyond mere chronological identification. Such identification was made by the words "in the days of Uzziah king of Judah" (v. 1). The added mention of the earthquake seems to be given as a divine portent of the awful judgment that was about to strike the Northern Kingdom in forty years—the 722 B.C. invasion by Assyria that would shake it to the ground and severely damage Judah.

Many fail to notice that the earthquake occurred two years *after* Amos saw his visions. Such a quake must have been received as a thunderclap of God confirming the prophesied doom. This cataclysm must have denied the words of those in Samaria who would have said, "That prophet was a fool; look around, everything is fine. God is not going to send any judgment out of heaven." Then came the boom. (Compare this with the 1980 Mt. St. Helens volcanic eruption that shook the United States.)

If Amos saw his vision first in 762 B.C. (his prophecy is generally dated 764-755 B.C.), then God would have given the Northern Kingdom exactly forty years warning to repent before the Assyrian invasion. In any case, the true figure assuredly approximates forty years and shows God's long-suffering. Earthquakes in the Bible often symbolize God's coming near for judgment. Thus they were seen at the giving of the law at Sinai (Exod. 19:18), and in the book of Revelation before impending calamities (Rev. 6:12; 8:5; 11:13, 19; 16:18-20).

"The LORD roars from Zion" (v. 2). The Hebrew word is *sha'ag*, which means "to roar like a lion" (see also Judg. 14:5). In Amos's day of complacency toward.open dishonesty, idolatry, and other sins, a bold and loud denunciation was necessary. God's lionlike roar here is the means of attempting to awaken those who are sleeping "at ease in Zion" (6:1) and those who "recline on beds of ivory" (6:4).

1. C. F. Keil and F. Delitzsch, *The Twelve Minor Prophets* (Grand Rapids: Eerdmans, n.d.), 1:234. This was originally published in 1861-68.

The imagery of verse 2 continues as it sees God's voice of judgment like a hot, windy blast that "dries up" the entire northern countryside, from the *lowland* grassy "shepherds' pasture grounds" to the lofty top of *high* Mt. Carmel, which stood 1, 677 feet above the adjacent Mediterranean Sea. Thus Amos tells of a judgment that is: (1) impending, about to strike, (2) thorough, from lowland to highland, and (3) devastating, leaving the once good lands dry and barren. As we look back in history and see what the wicked Assyrians did in their wholesale killings and wanton destructions, we see that this imagery is not merely poetic imagination, but actual history written in advance.

Amos 1:2 begins with words identical to Joel's words of sixty years before (Joel 3:16). In Joel, however, the lion's roar promises the end-time deliverance of Israel. Ironically, Amos uses these words of deliverance in an opposite sense and proclaims to those openly breaking God's holy law that His roar to them would not be one of deliverance, but rather one of destruction.

Does not much of society need to hear this message today? Liberals champion God's enduring love for all—even for those without conversion—and God's peace with the sinner as a result. People need to hear the words of Amos that warn the sinner to flee from the wrath to come, embrace Christ, and live.

II. Judgment Against the Heathen Nations (1:3–2:3)

From 1:3 to 2:16 God, through His prophet, proclaims judgment first against the six surrounding Gentile kingdoms (Syria, Gaza, Tyre, Edom, Ammon, Moab) and then against the two houses of Israel (Judah and Israel). Neither the Gentiles who are "without the Law" nor the Jewish people who are "under the Law" can escape the eye of God from heaven (Rom. 2:11-13). The time has come!

A. against syria (1:3-5)

"For three transgressions . . . and for four, I will not revoke its punishment" (v. 3). This identical formula, which has a rhythmic beat in the Hebrew, is used to introduce each of the offending nations to the punishment decrees (1:3, 6, 9, 11, 13; 2:1, 4, 6). It is much like Proverbs 6:16, which says, "There are

six things which the Lord hates, yes, seven." The idea seems
to be that the holy God has a plurality of adequate reasons,
in the case of each nation, for His punishing it; and if those
were not enough, He has even an extra reason to punish. The
heathen nations had repeatedly and continually sold themselves
to do evil—gross deeds of the cruelest and most heinous kind,
as we shall see in the descriptions that follow. Amid today's
"sympathetic-for-the-criminal" age, it should be a comfort to
know that God was not brandishing His avenging sword merely
because the named nations had committed their first slip (cf.
Gen. 15:16).

The word "transgressions" is the Hebrew *peshe,* which is
from the root *pasha,* meaning "to fall away, or break away from
anyone or thing; to turn away."[2] Hence, this word for sin emphasizes a *turning away* or *breaking away* from God's holy
standards of righteousness, goodness, fairness, and morality, as
comprehended in the Ten Commandments and His other laws.

Damascus (v. 3) is the capital of Syria, and it existed as far
back as 2000 B.C. It is the world's oldest continuously inhabited
city. It here represents the entire nation. The four sins that
God has in mind, for which He will now punish her, are not
listed. Rather, He has the prophet name only one of her most
heinous crimes, and in so doing the prophet allows us to see
clearly the gravity of Syria's crime and the malignity of the sin
that controlled her.

"Because they threshed Gilead with implements of sharp
iron" (v. 3). This refers to Syria's conquest of Gilead about
fifty years before, between 820-790 B.C. Today Gilead is called
Golani and is the Trans-Jordan land west of the Jordan River,
south of the Sea of Galilee, and north of the Dead Sea. In 2
Kings 10:32-33 and 13:3, 7 we read that Syria under kings
Hazael and Ben-hadad destroyed the Israelite army "and made
them like the dust of threshing." That was in the Syrian cam-
paign against Gilead and refers to the cruel ancient Syrian practice of riding over conquered prisoners, as well as the slain in
battle, with sharp-bladed iron threshing machines that would
chop and flay the bodies of the helpless victims.[3] Amos reveals

2. William Gesenius, *Hebrew and Chaldee Lexicon,* ed. S. P. Tregelles
   (Grand Rapids: Eerdmans, 1957), p. 695. This is a reprint of the
   monumental 1842 work.
3. Keil and Delitzsch, 1:243.

that God had witnessed that horrendous battlefield atrocity and would now mercilessly destroy merciless Syria. What a lesson is here for all in every age who have killed the Jews. Another lesson can be seen also. His eye is not only on the sparrow, but also on the deeds of sin, whether done openly or in secret.

"So I will send fire" (v. 4). Amos names two and possibly three Syrian kings: Ben-hadad I[4] (c. 890-841 B.C.), Hazael (841-801 B.C.), who murdered Ben-hadad I; and Ben-hadad II (801-785 B.C.). God's judgment against Syria historically fit the crime. The Syrians sought to enlarge their own nation by burning Israelite cities with fire, by pulling down the fortified citadels of Israel, by attempting population annihilation ("cut off the inhabitant," v. 5), and by forcing out into exile Israelites from Gilead (vv. 4-5). Their repayment would come to pass when powerful Assyria under Tiglath-pileser III would descend on Syria from the northeast in the campaigns of 743-738 B.C. (2 Kings 16:9). Fifty years later Isaiah reflected on Assyria's role and labeled her "the rod of My [God's] anger" (Isa. 10: 5-6).

"I will also break the gate bar of Damascus" (v. 5). The huge wooden beam that served to lock Damascus's gate at the time of a siege represents the strong human security possessed by this great city of antiquity. God would snap that bar, just as the cruel Syrian kings broke the bars of the Gilead cities they invaded. It is interesting to note that the word here for "break" is *shavar*, which is the word used in Genesis 19:9 for the wicked men of Sodom attempting "to break the door."

"From the valley of Aven . . . from Beth-eden" (v. 5). This valley of Aven is probably the Syrian valley that is thirty miles northwest of Damascus and that runs beside the heathen center of idolatry, Baalbek (here, Aven; later, Heliopolis). Beth-eden was a summer residence of the Syrian kings.[5]

God would yet cleanse that land of both idolatry and sinful pleasure.

"People of Aram will go exiled to Kir" (v. 5). Aram ("high region") is the ancient name for mountainous Syria. In 2 Kings

4. The name *Ben-hadad* means "Son-of Hadad." Hadad was the Syrian god of rainfall, and hence a fertility god.
5. Charles C. Ryrie, *The Ryrie Study Bible* (Chicago: Moody, 1978), p. 1359.

16:9 the fulfillment of this prophecy is explicitly stated, and the Syrians were exiled to Kir. This occurred in 732 B.C., when Tiglath-pileser III of Assyria killed Rezin, the king of Syria. The location of Kir is still unknown. Thus did the Lord fulfill His will against wicked Damascus. He threshed them who threshed His people.

B. AGAINST THE PHILISTINES (1:6-8)

The condemnation here is against the remnants of the Philistines who still had some strength and numbers in some of the southern coastal cities of Judah. This is confirmed by their being named in verse 8. During Amos's time the Philistines occupied four chief cities, namely those listed here: Gaza, Ashdod, Ashkelon, and Ekron. Keil claims that Gath was a fifth Philistine capital city, but the Philistines may have deserted the more inland Gath by this time.[6]

"They deported an entire population" (v. 6). The public incident of their sin, which is alluded to, is mentioned also in 2 Chronicles 21:16-17 and Joel 3:2-8. In the days of Jehoram (853-841 B.C.), a wicked king of Judah, the Philistines formed an alliance with the Phoenicians of Tyre to the north and with some of the Arab tribes to the south (2 Chron. 21:16; 22:1). They were successful in an invasion of Judah, and they carried off many captives, even including all but one of King Jehoram's sons and wives (2 Chron. 21:16-17). The Philistines and their allies then "deported an entire population" (v. 6). The Hebrew for this is *haglotam galut shelemah*, "they-made-naked making-naked completely," which is a typical Hebrew repetition idiom to express great force or thoroughness in an action. The additional words, "to deliver it up to Edom" (v. 6), show that the Philistine victors apparently sold their captive Jews to the nearby Edomites, who dwelled just south of the Dead Sea.

The Edomites, or Idumeans as they also were called, were from the lineage of Esau. They continually fought against Israel and Judah. At the time of this Philistine attack against Judah, when Jehoram was king of Judah, Edom was in active revolt against Jehoram. Prior to that, Jehoram's father, Jehoshaphat, had won a great victory (about 870 B.C.) over the Edomites and had subdued them for the next twenty years. (See

6. Keil and Delitzsch, 1:246-47.

2 Chron. 20:22-23, in which the Edomites are called "the inhabitants of Mount Seir.") The history of the Edomites shows them to be extremely cruel and filled with satanic hatred against the Jews.[7] In view of all this, we can see the magnitude of the sin that God used Amos to speak out against. When the Philistines won a victory over Judah and captured many people, they proceeded to sell their captive Jewish women and children into the hands of a cruel Jew-hating people. Whether the Philistines did that to further spite and torment the Jews, merely to obtain money, or to fulfill some prior demonic agreement with the Edomites, is not known.

For that sin God declared that He "will not revoke its punishment" (v. 6), which is part of the denunciation formula in each case. The Hebrew *Lo ashivenu* literally reads, "Not I-shall-turn-it," meaning that God had pronounced punishment and, because of the sin's evil, would not hold it back or turn it away. The sentence upon the Philistines in verses 7-8 declares that God would "cut off the inhabitant . . . and the remnant . . . will perish." So God pronounced the coming depopulation on the Philistines, who had sought to remove His ancient people from their land. God's justice is remarkable, whether it is meted out to individuals or nations. The punishments, when they arrive in His good time, fit the crime. How much better for nation and person to flee to Christ and get right with God (1 John 1: 9) than to wait for such an arrival of just deserts.

C. AGAINST TYRE (1:9-10)

The initial portion of the charge against Tyre, the Phoenician capital, is almost identical to the initial portion of the charge against the Philistines. And indeed Joel 3:4 confirms that both worked in league in the selling of Israelite captives to foreign nations. As already noted, verse 6 says the Philistines "deported an entire population" (*haglotam galut shelemah*; literally, "they-

---

7. The Edomite (Idumean) army in A.D. 69 was admitted into Jerusalem by a Zealot faction. The faction hoped the Edomites would drive out the other groups that were fighting each other in the city. Instead, after waiting outside all night in a rare cold and drenching rain, the Edomites turned against everyone in sight and killed multitudes of Jewish people. Josephus charges them with murdering 8,500, including two high priests. (Josephus *Wars of the Jews* 4.4.5. [Philadelphia: Winston, 1957 ed.].)

made-naked making-naked completely"). Here in verse 9 it reads, "They delivered up an entire population" (*hasgiram galut shelemah*; literally, "they-delivered-up making-naked completely"). The former phrase emphasizes the "making naked" of the land, that is, stripping it of people; however, the latter phrase focuses more on the delivering of the captives. Apparently the Phoenicians had participated more in the selling of the captive Jews than in the conquering of them or the taking of them off the land. That fits precisely with what we know about the Phoenicians. They were a maritime people, and their entire economy was built upon their sea trade. So, for money and perhaps a little hatred too, the merchants of Tyre had sold conquered Jews to the highest bidders. Joel 3:6 speaks of that trade and specifically names "the Greeks" (literally, "sons of Javan") as buyers of Jewish captives. Therefore some slaves must have been sold to the Greeks from time to time, whereas other Jewish captives, as here in Amos, were sold to the Edomites by both Phoenicians of Tyre and Philistines.

"And did not remember the covenant of brotherhood" (v. 9). The sin of Tyre's trafficking in Hebrew slaves was all the more heinous in light of the years of brotherly relations and nonaggression between the two nations. It was Hiram, the king of Tyre, who had participated so cordially and actively in the construction of both David's royal house and the Temple of Solomon (2 Sam. 5:11; 1 Kings 5:1, 7-18). Therefore judgment in verse 10, without any additional punishment as in the case of the other offending nations, fit Tyre's crime perfectly. Her "walls" and "citadels" (strong towers) would be consumed by the Lord, because she had cruelly turned against her brother nations Israel and Judah, whose walls and citadels she had helped to build years before. Why did she turn against her brother? The answer was, for the money that the trade in Jewish slaves brought from the west. God saw what Tyre had done, and He determined that the glorious outward symbols of Tyre's wealth, her city's walls and towers, would be torn down. That occurred from this time onward as Assyrians, Babylonians, Persians, Greeks, Egyptians, Seleucids, and finally the Romans (68 B.C.) besieged the city's walls and towers. The siege of Alexander in 332 B.C. took seven months and conquered the whole island city. It ended Phoenician commerical dominance of the eastern Mediterranean.

There is a lesson here that wealth obtained contrary to God's law will not prosper either a nation or an individual. In His good time and sovereign pleasure God will take such gain away.

D. AGAINST EDOM (1:11-12)

"Because he pursued his brother with the sword" (v. 11). The Edomites were the descendants of Esau, Jacob's brother, and, by that relationship of 1,000 years before, they were "brethren" to the Israelites. They are rebuked that even that consideration, their common blood descent from Isaac, had not held them back from murderous attacks upon Judah and Jerusalem.

"While he stifled his compassion" (v. 11). The inordinate reputation for cruelty that rested upon Edom has already been discussed along with verse 6. Here *shichet rachamayim,* "stifled his compassion," is literally "he-destroyed his-compassion," or "pity." Rather than focusing on one main evil event, the Lord gazes upon Edom's thousand-year history of hatred of her brother and mourns that Edom denied even the merciful impulses of conscience and "maintained his fury [anger, hatred, ill will] forever" (v. 11). There was simply no victory over this sin; it was a broken faucet of hatred that was never shut off. (See Num. 20:18; 2 Sam. 8:14; 2 Kings 8:20; 14:7.)

"So I will send fire upon Teman . . . Bozrah" (v. 12). The chief city or region of southern Edom was Teman (Jer. 49:7; Ezek. 25:13; Hab. 3:3), and the metropolis of northern Edom, famed for its dyed garments, was Bozrah (Isa. 34:6; 63:1; Jer. 49:13, 22). Thus God pronounced doom from one end to the other on an Edom that would not show mercy. What a lesson we see here against prolonged hatred and an unmerciful spirit (cf. Matt. 6:14-15).

E. AGAINST AMMON (1:13-15)

"Because they ripped open the pregnant women of Gilead" (v. 13). In this final section of chapter one, the judgments against Ammon are set forth. As the descendants of Lot, Abraham's nephew (Gen. 19:29-38), these people were also distant blood relatives to Israel. During the period of the judges the Ammonites confronted Jephthah with a claim that the land of Gilead (east of the Jordan River—today's western portion of the Hashamite Kingdom of Jordan) had belonged to them before Israel had entered the land (Judg. 11:12-30). That occurred about 1085 b.c., some 325 years before Amos's prophecy.[8]

Even though in other places the Bible does not mention explicitly the particular incident (or the series of incidents) alluded to in Amos, it was apparently one in which the Ammonites' murderous fury "to enlarge their borders" (v. 13) had known no bounds. Their lust for the land was backed by the ancient justification that it once had belonged to them, before Sihon took the land from them and before Israel took it from Sihon (Judg. 11:21-24). With that as their "moral" backing, they killed every Israelite in sight, including pregnant women. Is that not like so much in international affairs today? Because of some quasi-ethical claim, which may or may not have any justification, nations repeatedly claim righteousness to be on their side as they launch a war for an additional piece of land. With their claim they often proceed to justify every possible atrocity against the laws of God and man.

"Amid war cries" (v. 14). God saw what the Ammonites had done, and He did not buy their arguments of justification when His holy eyes beheld their atrocities against the women of Gilead. Therefore God would punish Ammon. Amid crying and shouts for mercy, amid "storm on the day of tempest" (wild, unrelenting brutality), the murderers of Ammon would themselves be destroyed. Even as they killed Gilead's fruit of the womb, her hope for the future, so God would also take away the royal family of Ammon (v. 15), which was Ammon's hope for the future.

Four lessons can be learned from God's dealing with Ammon: (1) even the wicked justify their aggressive acts and wars; (2) the mere declaration of war does not justify atrocities against civilians; (3) God sees the atrocities that occur, even in the chaos of the battlefield; and (4) that person or nation who advances himself wickedly, at the expense of others, ultimately will be demoted by the Lord God.

8. John C. Whitcomb, Jr., *Chart of the Old Testament Kings and Prophets* (Chicago: Moody, 1968), p. 1.

Ezekiel 25:5 and Zephaniah 2:9 also prophetically pronounce desolation on Ammon, and that has been fulfilled. "Nothing but ruins are found here by the amazed explorer. Not an inhabited village remains, and not an Ammonite exists on the face of the earth."[9]

F. AGAINST MOAB (2:1-3)

Following the previous pattern, the Lord declares that He is condemning Moab not merely for the single act named, but for at least three capital offenses and, with further examination, four.

"Because he burned the bones of the king of Edom to lime" (v. 1). It is suggested that that event may have occurred in connection with the war of 2 Kings 3 (c. 850 B.C.), some ninety years before Amos prophesied. At that time Moab was in tributary status to Israel. When Israel's King Ahab died, Moab rebelled. During that war Ahab's son Joram secured the help of Jehoshaphat of Judah and the king of Edom, who at that moment was friendly to Judah and her good king Jehoshaphat. Moab's king and army were trapped, and they tried to break out through the line at which the king of Edom held his troops. They failed because Edom's army held its position. In desperation the king of Moab sacrificed his own eldest son and heir upon a high wall to Chemosh, the Moabite national deity. Apparently that act so sickened everyone that the war was abandoned (2 Kings 3:26-27).

We may conjecture that the above-mentioned incident so filled the king of Moab with hatred against the king of Edom that some time later Moab brutally attacked Edom. During the battle the fierce hatred of the Moabites apparently knew no bounds and was culminated by the burning of the bones of the dead king of Edom. Amos 2:1 does not say that he was burned alive.

Thus Moab's sin seems to have been the sin of implacable hatred, shown by a grudge keeping that is not satisfied simply with an enemy's death but that wishes to burn his bones also. The entire incident points up the evils of: (1) human sacrifice, and (2) hatred that endures. (See Lev. 19:17; Matt. 5:44; Luke

9. William M. Thompson, *The Land and the Book*, 3 vols. (New York: Harper and Bros., 1880), 3:622.

6:27; and for a New Testament example of implacable hatred, Rev. 17:16.)

"So I will send fire upon Moab, and it will consume the citadels of Kerioth (v. 2). The word *citadels* is *ar'minot* ("high places"), hence fortresses, palaces, or walled fortifications; and *Kerioth* is literally "cities"—quite possibly a proper name of a city in Moab (Isa. 15:1), which Ryrie suggests might have been the capital.[10] Moab had wickedly burned the bones of those whom she hated, and God will utterly burn and devour her cities. The worship of Chemosh by the Moabites, like the worship of Molech by the Canaanites, called for human sacrifice, which was usually a child (2 Kings 3:27). That worship was often accomplished with the beating of drums and with the use of other loud instruments—perhaps to drown out the shrieks of the children. To a nation that slays its own and burns others' bones, God announces that His judgment will slay such a nation's people amid trumpets and shouts of His making.

"I will also cut off the judge" (v. 3). The judges of Moab, who have no better judgment than to tolerate such evils as human sacrifice, will be cut off by God (cf. Rev. 3:16). Here the Hebrew parallelism is noted: "cut off . . . judge" and "slay princes." To Moab, whose insatiable leaders would not settle for anything but total annihilation of her enemies, God promises that He will now demand a likewise thorough purging upon those who decreed annihilation to others (cf. Matt. 7:2). All of this occurred by the hands of the soon-conquering Assyrians and Babylonians.

---

10. Ryrie, p. 1360.

8

INGRATES ARE JUDGED BY GOD

With Moab, 2:1-3 concludes the condemnations of the heathen. If men of Israel were amid the crowds that heard the denunciations of the six Gentile nations, those Israelites must have fallen instantly in love with the rugged prophet from Tekoa. But, when he proceeded to launch into similar diatribes against Judah and Israel, their love must have transformed itself into acrimony. The second chapter of Amos marks that transition of turning from scolding the Gentiles to scolding the Jews.

III. JUDGMENT AGAINST GOD'S CHOSEN PEOPLE (2:4-16)

A. AGAINST JUDAH (2:4-5)

"Because they rejected the law of the Lord" (v. 4). Here the Lord does not cite any particularly heinous deed of Judah, as He did in His condemnations of the Gentile nations, but the focus is upon Judah's *rejection* of God's revelation, His sacred law. The Hebrew word *ma'as* means "to reject, to despise, to have an aversion for, to condemn, to have contempt for." The expression "the law of the Lord" is *Torah Yahweh. Torah* denotes God's written commandments, including the entire set of Mosaic books, the Pentateuch. Amos's testimony is that Judah as a nation both actively repudiated God's law and passively despised it by not keeping it—ignoring it and disobeying it. Read Romans 2:11-13, 17-29, which gives a divinely inspired, eloquent commentary on this charge by God against His own nation Judah, the nation out of which Messiah would someday come. (See also Lev. 26:14-16, 31, which is Moses' prophecy of the consequences if God's people rejected His law.)

Notice in verse 4 the progression of God's three charges against Judah: first, the despising of His holy and life-giving

law; second, the consequent breaking of His commandments
and regulations concerning worship and life; and third, the
consequent self-deception that the ignoring of God's regulations did not really matter much in daily living. That triple
error brought the divine wrath upon Judah. For that error the
"citadels of Jerusalem" would be ruined (v. 5). The noun
armon means "high tower, fortress, the strongest point in a
palace or castle, citadel."[1] The citadels of Jerusalem were dam-
aged and finally destroyed by the Babylonian invasions under
Nebuchadnezzar in 606 B.C., 597 B.C., and 586 B.C. In 586 the
Temple of Solomon was looted, torn down, burned, and the
city itself finally razed, all its wall towers being pulled down
to the ground by great Babylonian ropes (2 Chron. 36:11-20).
Thus Amos's prophecy was fulfilled.

Note 1: The incident of 2 Chronicles 26:16-23 describes an act
of Uzziah, who was the king of Judah during Amos's prophecy. If Dr. John C. Whitcomb's chart is correct, in 750 B.C.
Uzziah despised God's law and attempted to offer incense in
the Temple, which only a priest of Levi was permitted to do.
For that, God struck Uzziah with leprosy, and his son Jotham
had to take over the duties of king. Uzziah's sinful act would
have occurred at the end of Amos's ministry, or within five
years of the end. It certainly confirms God's charge given in
Amos 2:4 that Judah despised God's law; the king merely
did as he pleased until God struck him down.

Note 2: God could have fulfilled his sentence against Judah and
Jerusalem in 701 B.C. when Sennacherib invaded with his
huge Assyrian army of 185,000. At that time the Assyrians
took captive the Northern Kingdom and then moved their
army to capture Jerusalem and Judah. However, Hezekiah,
that righteous king of Judah, prayed to God for forgiveness
and deliverance, and God in His sovereign grace spared Jerusalem and destroyed the Assyrian army (Isa. 37). God thus
waited until the rise of Babylon and in 586 B.C. fulfilled all
of Amos's prophecy so literally. Hezekiah's prayer stayed the
judgment for more than a century. (Cf. James 5:16-18.)

B. AGAINST ISRAEL (2:6-16)

It is impossible to know Amos's location when he saw each

1. William Gesenius, *Hebrew and Chaldee Lexicon,* ed. S. P. Tregelles
(Grand Rapids: Eerdmans, 1957), p. 80.

vision and spoke or wrote each prophecy. From 7:12-13, however, where he is told to go back to Judah and from Amos's
frequent allusions to Samaria (the capital of the North), we
may safely surmise, along with most commentators, that his
prophetic ministry was primarily to Samaria and the Northern
Kingdom (3:9; 4:1; 6:1; 8:14).[2] Amos turns at last to point
the Lord's rebuke at a strong, wealthy, and uncaring Israel,
which was ruled by the mighty Jeroboam II.

1. *Israel's waywardness* (2:6-8)

As in the case of the previous nations judged, the Lord declares that Israel's penalty will not be remitted. That is because God again has more than sufficient grounds for her punishment, namely, "For three transgressions . . . and for four"
(v. 6). Through Amos, God then proceeds to list at least seven
specific sins of the nation. In the previous seven condemnations
of the various nations, only one or two sins were listed for each,
and those stood as sufficient to display the wicked character of
each condemned people. Here, however, the prophet releases
a flood of condemnations, as if the dam of longsuffering had
finally burst.

"Because they sell the righteous for money and the needy for
a pair of sandals" (v. 6). Here we see the people's crimes of
perverting justice and dealing harshly with their fellow Israelites for the sake of financial gain. "The righteous" refers to "the
righteous person" (Hebrew, *tsaddik*) and is the same root word
from which the New Testament group *Tsadikim* (or in Greek,
Sadducees, "righteous ones") springs. Keil suggests that here
Amos speaks of the practice of judges' accepting bribes in legal
cases to overturn the causes of righteous people.[3] It may also
speak of the selling of good and decent people into slavery because of a debt. The selling of "the needy for a pair of sandals"
would refer to the selling of poor people into slavery because of
debts they acquired on the lowliest of life's necessities. What
harsh and mean people Israel had become, and the growing
wealth of Samaria made such a sin all the worse. (See Lev.
25:39 and 2 Kings 4:1 on enslavement for debt.) The parable of

2. See again the section on Samaria in the Introduction, pp. 83-86.
3. Cf. Keil and F. Delitzsch, *The Twelve Minor Prophets* (Grand Rapids: Eerdmans, n.d.), 1:252-53.

the unmerciful servant in Matthew 18:23-35, especially verses 32-34, gives the Lord's view on those who have been forgiven much and who then treat their own brethren unmercifully.

It should be observed that Amos rebukes the nations not merely for one kind of sin, but for sins of every class: for *theological errors*, that is, false belief and idolatry (3:14); for *cruelty in warfare and conquest* (1:13); for *breaking His moral law* (2:7); and here for *social evils*, oppressing the poor (2:6).

"These who pant after the very dust of the earth on the head of the helpless" (v. 7). The word *pant* is *sha-af*. The latter part of it, *-af*, means "nose, nostrils, anger," and the entire word means "to sniff the ground as an animal in chase of prey." This condemnation could mean (1) the wicked sniffed the ground like dogs in pursuit of their helpless victims, or (2) the wicked begrudged the helpless even the dust of mourning, which they marked on their foreheads (Job 2:12 [Hitzig's view]), or (3) the wicked anxiously desired to see the dust of grief upon the heads of the afflicted (2 Sam. 1:2 [Keil's view]).[4] In any case, it is absolutely clear that the oppressors had zeal in heaping grief upon the heads of the helpless. And God's condemnation of that is equally clear.

"And a man and his father resort to the same girl . . . to profane my holy name" (v. 7). The word *resort* in the Hebrew is *halach*, which merely means "to go, to walk." The picture was one of such widespread immorality that different generations of the same family were illicitly involved with the same woman (possibly a temple prostitute, although the Hebrew says simply *na-ar*, "young girl"). That a man and his father both commit sin with the same woman shows that living in sin is here not an isolated case of only one person's falling, but rather entire families are pictured as having been corrupted. The corruption may have become so much a part of society that father and son no longer hid their sin from one another, contrary to the normal aim of father and son to appear at least outwardly upright before one another. The result was the profaning of God's holy name.

The expression "in order to profane my holy name" (v. 7), begins in the Hebrew with the preposition *li-ma'an*, used to

4. Ibid. Hitzig and Keil were two of the great scholars of the last century.

express purpose and intention. The prophet speaks with irony, declaring that these notorious sinners so flaunt their sin that they seem to be purposely aiming at degrading God's holy name among the heathen who observe them.

"Beside every alter . . . they drink the wine of those who have been fined" (v. 8). The people reached a new height of sinfulness, probably beside the two religious altars with golden calves at Bethel and Dan. They assembled themselves in comfort, amid garments that were received as pledges for the repayment of debts. Thus the supposed scenes of religious piety, as places where their financial oppressors gathered, would become abhorent to the poor; the oppressors would stand under the shadow of the altars of the Lord and His legal backing for their unremittingly shrewd and harsh dealings with debtors. (See Exod. 22:25; Deut. 24:12-13.) The beverage of that "pious community" was probably the tasty wine purchased with the revenues from the religious lawyers' fines against the people. Keil suggests that because this wine was consumed in the house of God, feast days are in mind here.[5] We note that the blatant sin of the day had made its inroads even into the house of God, the very place in which it should have been condemned. Here sinners gathered to drink and boast—in pious terms to be sure— of their wickedness; and they felt comfortable, apparently because they were under the shelter of the altars. No wonder that God disowned them with the words "the house of *their* God" (v. 8, italics added); and no wonder that He had to go to Tekoa in the south to find a righteous man to rebuke them. (Cf. Ezek. 34:1-10; Matt. 23:4, 14, 27; Luke 10:13-16; 11:46; 14:3-6.)

2. *God's past blessings on Israel* (2:9-11)

Israel had deserted her God in *a supreme act of ingratitude*. Her people had sinned against Him openly despite His: (1) destruction of the strong Amorite armies that had been before them in Canaan, verse 9, (2) His deliverance of them from a life of slavery in Egypt, verse 10, (3) His providing for their needs in a wilderness migration, which normally would have claimed all of their lives in famine and disease, verse 10, (4) His bringing them into the promised land and giving it to them

5. Ibid., 1:254.

by many miracles, verse 10, and (5) His providing for their religious and ethical welfare in manifestations of His presence and guidance through spokesmen and prophets, such as no other nation had ever experienced, verse 11.

"Then I raised up . . . prophets . . . Nazirites" (v. 11). Here the causative form of the verb is used in the Hebrew: *ah-kim,* "I caused to rise," followed by "from your sons." From this we learn that true prophets were called by God—the initiation of the call came from Him (see 7:14-15; Exod. 3:4, 10-12; Jer. 1:4-10; Acts 26:16; 2 Peter 1:21). False prophets were those seers who spoke in God's name the imaginings of their own hearts (Jer. 23:21). This truth is not accepted by the liberals and unbelievers who view all religion as the invention and imaginations of men. (See Mark 5:41, where Jesus used the same Hebrew verb *kum.* See also Amos 2:11, "*I raised up*" [italics added].)

This entire passage shows that God knows the bounty of blessing that He has bestowed on each of us and upon our nation. Our sins therefore appear all the worse, because they represent ingratitude for His many blessings.

3. *Israel's perfidy* (2:12-13)

"But you made the Nazirites drink wine . . . commanded the prophets . . . 'You shall not prophesy!' " (v. 12). Here is one of the most profound verses in the Old Testament. The background of it is Numbers 6:1-21, which forbids the Nazirite to drink wine. The liberals in America in the 1920s and 1930s, and in Europe a half-century before, made many of our would-be Nazirites (preachers) "drunk" with their Bible-denying teachings. They robbed them of their holy office and perverted their ministries throughout an entire generation. The liberals did all that in the same way as the wicked in Israel enticed the holy men, whom God had raised up to teach and rebuke the nation, to fall and join them in their consuming sins. Just as wine defiles the Nazirite, unbelieving liberalism defiles the preacher. (Cf. Judg. 16:16-22; Luke 1:15.)

In a parallel action, Israel not only refused the message of the prophets but in sinful scorn also commanded them to be silent. Our Lord's words provide the best commentary here (Matt. 23:13, 29-39).

"As a wagon is weighted down" (v. 13). God describes by a vivid picture His feelings of abused longsuffering. The portrait is one of His having borne a great deal of evil from the people of Israel. They had filled up the full measure of His patience. Their sins had reached His straining and breaking point, and He could bear no more—judgment was about to fall. (Cf. Matt. 23:35-36; 1 Cor. 11:30; Eph. 4:30.)

4. *Israel's judgment certain* (2:14-16)

All the things described here refer to an army that no longer will have God fighting with it or for it. All success and blessing will flee; defeat will replace victory at every hand. This is the punishment of powerlessness that grips the blessed of God as long as they forsake His ways. What is the remedy? 1 John 1:9. (Cf. Deut. 28:15-68; Josh. 7:3-13; Judg. 16:20-22; Matt. 22:1-7).

Verses 14-15 not only do not speak of future military victories for strong but sinful Israel, they rather speak of devastating future defeats. The defeats, resulting from God's withdrawal of blessing, will be so disastrous and overwhelming that these final three verses of the chapter repeat over and over that escape will be impossible. In verse 14 it is said that neither (1) speed, (2) bravery ("stalwart"), nor (3) strength ("mighty") will save a man. Verse 15 likewise announces that neither (1) weapons ("bow"), (2) speed in running away, nor (3) having a horse will enable one to escape. At best, according to verse 16, the "bravest" will escape "naked." Within forty years all would be fulfilled at the hands of the invading Assyrians. O that men might see and realize the awful penalty that befalls nations that forsake God. Even the strongest nations, when they abandon God, fall swiftly and totally.

What a lesson we can learn from the ingratitude of a uniquely blessed people as reported in Amos 2. It is worth noting that at the end of the 1970s preachers all over the United States launched repeatedly into a common theme, namely, that the United States's military failures and "ill luck" at that time were results of God's providential hand of blessing being withheld from a nation where sin was (and still is) increasing and the fear of God declining.

9

GOD'S OWN BLESSED PEOPLE ARE JUDGED BY HIM

IV. Amos's Sermons Against Israel (3:1–6:14)

A. JUDGMENT ANNOUNCED AGAINST ISRAEL (3:1-8)

1. *The betrothal of Israel to God* (3:1-2)

"Against the entire family which He brought up from the land of Egypt" (v. 1). Continually throughout the Old Testament God's deliverance of Israel from Egyptian slavery is cited as a foundation for the special relationship between God and Israel (Exod. 20:2; Deut. 5:6; Psalm 78:12-16). Because He redeemed them from the house of bondage, they belonged to Him in a unique way. He was to be their God, and they were to be His people and keep His covenant of the law, the Ten Commandments, and all the statutes that accompanied it.

Thus, in Hosea 2:2 and following Israel is admonished as the wife of Jehovah who has not been faithful to her husband. In the same way believers in Jesus, the church, are the Bride of Christ and belong in a unique way to the Lord on the ground of Christ's substitutionary redemption. The church therefore owes Him love and faithfulness (2 Cor. 11:2; Rev. 19:7-9).

"You only have I chosen among all the families of the earth" (v. 2). In the Hebrew these words read, "Only you I have known from all families of the earth." The verb *yada'*, "to know," can mean: (1) to know, in the sense of perception, *intellectual understanding*, or cognition, and (2) to know, in the sense of experiencing, becoming *intimately acquainted* with someone—a knowing of fellowship (cf. Gen. 4:1; Ezek. 6:7). Some have been puzzled over the King James translation of this verse and have asked themselves, "How could God say that He knew *only* Israel? Surely He *knew* everything and knew that other nations existed!" What God is really saying is that, among all the nations ("families") on the globe, Israel ("you") is the only one that He has known *in fellowship and intimacy.* God personally gave Israel the Ten Commandments, appeared to her prophets, spoke to Abraham and Moses, and was present at the Tabernacle in the wilderness. Now, after all that, both the Northern and Southern Kingdoms of Israel had deserted Him and run off as unfaithful wives to Baal. The Northern Kingdom's desertion, however, was more advanced at this time; therefore judgment would fall on her first and heaviest (Hosea 1:6-7; 3:4).

2. *The bisection of Israel from God* (3:3)

"Do two men walk together unless they have made an appointment?" (v. 3). The exact meaning of this verse is much argued over by commentators. Its Hebrew reads, "Do they walk two together, except if they-have-made-an-agreement-to-meet?" The final verb is *no-ad,* "to meet by appointment" (Neh. 6:2, 10; Job 2:11).[1] Many of the commentators, including Cocceius, the seventeenth-century Dutch theologian, have believed that the two men were the Lord and the nation of Israel.[2] The King James translation probably favors this view: "Can two walk together, except they be agreed?" So here the thought of verse 2 continues as God declares that He can no longer walk with Israel because they, He and Israel, are no longer in agreement regarding where to meet or in which direction to walk. A different view is taken by Keil, who sees this verse as beginning the next section and speaking of the meeting between Amos and God. According to this view, Amos would not be speaking for God and breathing out judgments if he and God had not met by God's call.[3] Both explanations fit the context and are reasonable, however I favor the first view. A *bisection* of the union between God and Israel has taken place.

3. *The prophet's bemoaning of the separation* (3:4-8)

"Does a lion roar? . . . Does a young lion growl? . . . Does a bird fall?" (vv. 4-5). First, by two parallel metaphors pictur-

1. William Gesenius, *Hebrew and Chaldee Lexicon,* ed. S. P. Tregelles (Grand Rapids: Eerdmans, 1957), p. 355.
2. C. F. Keil and F. Delitzsch, *The Twelve Minor Prophets* (Grand Rapids: Eerdmans, n.d.), 1:260.
3. Ibid.

ing lions, the prophet announces that the Lord already has Israel
in His grasp for punishment. The adult lion (*aryeh*) gives his
triumphant roar when he smells the prey and is about to start
his final pursuit. Then, in Bochart's words, comes the "slaughter
and laceration."[4] The young lion (*kafir*) growls from his den
when the prey is already his. (See also Isa. 5:29; Hos. 11:10.)

Lions inhabited Palestine until about A.D. 80 when the Romans removed them for the gladiatorial shows and persecutions,
which culminated in the dedication ceremonies of the Roman
Colosseum in that year. (See Judg. 14:5-6; 1 Sam. 17:34-35 concerning lions.)

Note 1: Israel's recently developed (1978) small jet fighter
plane has been named the *Kafir*, or "Young Lion."

Both metaphors describing traps in verse 5 also say that the
Lord already has Israel in His grasp for judgment. The Northern Kingdom is the bird, and the bait is the people's sinfulness.
God's punishment is the trap of divine justice in which Israel
is now caught.

"If a trumpet is blown . . . will not the people tremble?" (v.
6). Here Amos is admonishing his hearers that his trumpetlike
warning message is one received from the Lord, at which the
people of Israel ought to tremble. The implication is that they
should repent. Amos further assures his listeners that the calamity to come upon their city will be from the Lord Himself.

"His servants the prophets" (v. 7). The English word
prophet comes from the Greek *pro-phāmi*, "for-to speak," one
who speaks on behalf of another. In Scripture it was a holy man
called of God, filled with His Spirit, who spoke the words that
God would have him speak (2 Tim. 3:16; 2 Pet. 1:21). Thus in
Exodus 7:1 Moses is compared to God, and Moses' spokesman
Aaron, who speaks to Pharaoh what Moses tells him to say, is
called Moses' prophet. (See also Exod. 4:15-16.) The Hebrew
word for prophet is *navi*, which comes from the verb root *nava*,
"to cause to bubble, to pour forth with words, hence to speak
prophetically."[5]

That the prophets are here called "His servants" further il-
lustrates the truth that the prophets of the Bible were not

4. Ibid.
5. Gesenius, pp. 525, 526-28.

merely self-inspired, self-motivated religious enthusiasts, as unbelievers have often claimed. On the contrary, they *served God* by speaking His words as He gave them voice (2 Peter 1:20-21). So Jesus, the great Prophet, claimed continually that the words He spoke were the very words given Him by the Father to speak (e.g. John 14:24; 17:8).

Amos gives a general maxim that "the Lord God does nothing unless He reveals His secret counsel to His servants the prophets" (v. 7). The word *reveals* in the Hebrew is *gala*, which has the root meaning "to uncover"; hence it means "to reveal" a secret. Likewise *secret counsel* represents the single word *sōd*, which means a "couch or cushion," and hence a secret told by one whispering to another while sitting closely together.[6]

This verse must mean that in the realm of great national judgments, which in that period would fall upon the nations of Israel and Judah, God definitely and consistently used the prophets to announce what judgments would befall those nations and why.

"A lion has roared! . . . The Lord God has spoken! Who can but prophesy?" (v. 8). If a lion (*aryeh*, "adult lion") roars, that means he is about to rush toward his prey and devour it. Animal and human victims alike would normally fall into a paralyzing fear at such a sound of impending doom. Amos implies that this should be the reaction of Israel at the Lord's warning (1:2). But he also has another reaction, namely, that when the Lord communicates such a judgment to the prophet, the prophet has a holy, unquenchable duty and impulse to give voice to the divine message. Jeremiah 20:9 is an eloquent and powerful commentary on this truth. Certainly there are two complementary lessons in Amos 3:8: (1) when God speaks a warning by His Word, we do well to heed it, and (2) we too, as His witnesses, should warn the lost of their souls' perilous condition and of the necessity for them to flee to the Savior for forgiveness and life.

B. SAMARIA'S COMING DOOM (3:9-15)

1. *The prophet summons the enemies* (3:9)

"Proclaim on the citadels in Ashdod and . . . in the land of

6. Ibid., pp. 170, 580.

Egypt and say, 'Assemble yourselves on the mountains of
Samaria'" (v. 9). Here Amos powerfully personifies the enemies of Israel and summons them to investigate and witness the
situation in the Northern Kingdom. He invites those who are
afar off to witness the "great tumults" (*mehumot,* "disturbances,
wild living"). Proverbs 15:16 has this same Hebrew word. The
enemies are also invited to view "the oppressions" (*ashukim,*
"injuries due to violence") that were to be found daily in
Samaria, which was built upon the mountains of Ephraim. So
Amos cries that the whole world ought to understand what sins
had occurred in Samaria, which sins had now caught up with
her and had resulted in God's proclamation that her time of
judgment had at last arrived. (Cf. Rev. 18:4-8.)

2. *The belligerence of the people of Samaria* (3:10)

"But they do not know how to do what is right" (v. 10).
Now we are supplied with a basic reason for God's summoning
judgment upon them. The expression "what is right" is a translation of the Hebrew *nachoach,* meaning "straight," from the
root "to go straight."[7] Those people in Samaria, in the language
of modern-day law enforcers, "do not know how to go straight."
Why? Because they had corrupted the true message and religion of God, which He had sent to teach them how to go
straight. We have already been told this in Amos 2:8, 11-12.
Israel's religious centers had become places of corruption instead of deliverance (2:8), and the prophets whom God had
raised up for Israel had been shouted into silence, except for
Elijah and Elisha—and the people resisted them so strenuously
(2:11-12).[8]

My father was a wise, plain-speaking man of yesteryear, much
like I imagine Amos to have been. In our Philadelphia grocery
store he was robbed five times—at gunpoint, at knifepoint, when
a brick shattered the glass, when a door was smashed in, and
when shoved into a car. He said to me often, much like Amos
in this verse, "Gary, these people don't know how to be honest,
even if they wanted to be." The sin habit, persisted in, had be-

---

7. Ibid., p. 550.
8. The prophets of the Northern Kingdom in that era were Elijah (c.
850 B.C.), Elisha (c. 840), Jonah (c. 780), Amos (c. 760), and
Hosea (c. 752-722).

come the unalterable way of life, and only the power of God could break it.

"Who hoard up violence and devastation" (v. 10). The fact that they "hoard up [*atzar*, "store up, heap up, pile up in a safe place"] violence and devastation" shows that God was not indicting them with charges of mere technical slips in their observances of His many ceremonial laws. He rather accuses them of being such confirmed, gross sinners and such oppressors of their fellowmen that they were heaping up records of violence and sin for which God must judge them (cf. Prov. 10: 12; Isa. 33:5-6; Luke 12:21; James 5:3).

In light of all this, the words "they do not know how to do what is right" must be understood to signify that the people of Samaria now had such seared consciences that they no longer even *knew* (*yada'*, same word as in 3:2) what was right in the sight of God. (Cf. Rom. 3:9-18.)

3. *The banishment of Samaria and Israel* (3:11-15)

Israel, having turned her back on so many unique blessings from God (2:9-11; 3:1-2), and having now reached a position of confirmed, daily sin in false religion and oppression (2:6-8; 3:10), is a nation marked by God for calamity and national punishment. That punishment is described here in verses 11-15.

"An enemy . . . surrounding . . . will pull down your strength . . . your citadels will be looted (v. 11). The Assyrians under Shalmaneser V came in 724 B.C. and besieged the city of Samaria for three years. King Hoshea of Israel had attempted to revolt against paying the Assyrians the annual tribute money they had demanded. He had made a treaty with the pharaoh of Egypt to help him, but the pharaoh did not come to help (2 Kings 18: 21). Samaria collapsed in 722 B.C. Now under Sargon II, who had seized power in 721 B.C., the Assyrians pulled down the towers and took 27,290 of the people captive.[9] Sargon then placed an Assyrian ruler over the city, looted it of fifty royal chariots and various other items, and levied the former tribute on it. Sargon then began to implement the infamous Assyrian policy of mixing conquered peoples to keep them from being

9. *The Inscriptions of Sargon II, Part I, The Annals* (Paris, 1929), quoted in J. B. Pritchard, ed., *The Ancient Near East* (Princeton, N.J.: U. Press, 1958), p. 195.

able to organize a revolt. Thus the Assyrians took the 27,000 Israelites out of the city and mixed them into Persian cities and other areas. At the same time, the Assyrians brought other foreigners into Samaria from far off captive regions. That policy eventually produced the mixed, quasi-Jewish population that was characteristic of the Samaritans of Christ's time (John 4: 20-22). The story of Samaria's fall is recounted in detail in 2 Kings 17.

It is proper to note that Assyria's actions basically ended Samaria as a capital city and ended the Northern Kingdom's existence as a separate nation. Thus the nation of Israel, which appeared almost forever invincible when Amos preached to Jeroboam II in 760 B.C., was to cease being a nation within forty years after the prophet's words of doom. Amos's words are still appropriate: "A lion has roared! Who will not fear?" (3:8).

Note 2: The British Israelite theory advocates that the ten tribes that constituted the Northern Kingdom were "the Lost Tribes of the House of Israel." They, according to the theory, were driven out of Samaria en masse in 722-721 B.C. by the Assyrians. Then for a thousand years they wandered into Eastern and then Western Europe, and finally about the eighth century A.D., after 1,500 years of lost wandering, ended up in northwestern Europe, chiefly in Britain, northern France, and the Scandinavian countries. Thus, it is said, the queen of England is today the true ruler of Israel, and the blessed British and Americans (who migrated from Britain) are the "true Israel" and will inherit the Old Testament promises of God's eventual end-time restoration of Israel! The Jews, it is maintained, are from the tribe of Judah, but they have been mixed with other groups, especially the Khazars (an ancient Turkish people, who lived north of the Black Sea. The Khazar nobility converted to Judaism in the eighth century A.D., but the nation fell at the end of the tenth century A.D.).

The end result of this theory casts aspersions on the true identity of today's Jewish people and claims that the end-time restoration of them to the land is intended more for the British than for today's Zionists. The advocates of this theory are often anti-Semitic beyond what many would believe to be humanly possible. An exception would be the Worldwide Church of God (Armstrongism), which does not show traces of anti-Semitism or anti-Zionism and seems to be pro-Israel. The theory, however, is devoid of any historical evidence of support and is actually contrary to history. For example, note the following: (1) history witnesses that the ten tribes people from Samaria maintained much of their Hebrew culture and religion through the years, though scattered, (2) biblical and historical indications universally testify of the scattering of those Israelites from Samaria, rather than their remaining together, (3) there has been no evidence whatsoever of so large a group as those of the ten tribes, called "Israelites" or any other name, staying together on a 1,500-year pilgrimage across Europe, (4) no serious British, biblical, or Jewish historian anywhere at anytime has given credence to the theory, and (5) the Bible and secular history record a mixing of the Jews of Judah with the Israelites from Samaria after 586 B.C. when Jerusalem fell to the Babylonians. Then all the Jewish people were again scattered. Personally and honestly, I believe this theory to be a lie of Satan to cause further persecution upon the Jewish people, to undermine all claims to their ancient land, and to deceive both the simple and evil minded.

"From the lion's mouth . . . a piece of an ear" (v. 12). Here the prophet declares that the nation of Israel will be pulled to pieces, just as the devouring and ripping lion cuts away and separates chunks of flesh. What a perfect prophetic picture of the fate the Assyrians were going to levy upon the nation. Assyria tore away chunks of captives and spread the pieces around Asia, Europe, and Africa. (See Deut. 28:49-51, 63-68.)

"Snatched away with the corner of a bed" (v. 12). The ivory-inlaid beds and couches of Samaria would be taken away, along with the people. Amos 6:4 speaks of those costly ivory ornaments, and the "cover of a couch" (3:12) refers to fancy woven quilts and pillows imported from Damascus, capital of Syria. The word translated "cover" is *Damasc* in the Hebrew and refers to such items of pillowed luxury that that city produced and exported.[10] Thus, those who rejected God, in spite

10. Keil and Delitzsch, 1:264.

of so many blessings, were to be pulled by the Assyrian beast from downy beds of consummate luxury to servitude, degradation, persecution, and shame (Isa. 10:6).

"I will also punish the altars of Bethel" (v. 14). The coming destruction would finally take care of the problem of the two ungodly centers of worship, Bethel and Dan, where Jeroboam I had long before set up the great dual altars topped by golden calves (1 Kings 12:26-33). After two full centuries (922-722 B.C.) of preaching, with both Elijah and Elisha rebuking sin in the north, those two altars of abomination still stood. The Hebrew word translated twice in this verse as "punish" is *pakad,* and is translated "visit" both times in the King James Version. The root idea of this verb is *to convey movement toward something,* hence, "to strike, visit" (in a good sense, 1 Samuel 17: 18), or "to punish." The choice of this verb is most appropriate. Here "the altars of Bethel" were clearly altars that God hated and from which His blessed presence was absent (see 1 Kings 12:27–13:5). Now at last it is announced that God would "visit" (*pakad*) them; however this visit by God would be one of punishment and destruction, rather than one wherein He was heeding the prayers of the repentant of Israel.

The longsuffering of God had apparently expired, and it was only through the violence of the Assyrian conquest that Israel would get the message that the two altars had to come down. (See Isaiah 28:11. In Isaiah a century and a half later it was Judah who would not "get the message" until God spoke to her by bringing conquering Babylonian troops to the land [28:14 ff.]. Then she too understood. Cf. 1 Corinthians 14:21.)

It is not amiss to note that the United States, at one time the world's bastion for freedom, what is right, and the sending of missionaries around the globe, also has reached its two-century mark. Godlessness seems to be on the rise, and one can only pray that this great nation will not repeat the folly of Israel, and that the worldwide forces of Communism will not be her Assyria.

"Winter . . . summer house" (v. 15). Kings and wealthy people often had two main residences. I have a wealthy friend, an outstanding Christian, and he and his wife reside in one part of the United States for the summer, and then at their other house for the winter. The kings of the ancient Middle East did this. Herod the Great, for example, often went for the hot summers to his lofty palace 1,450 feet atop Masada (by the Dead Sea). Here, precisely as high as New York's 102-story Empire State Building, cool breezes wafted over him when he wearied of the hot baths installed in the Roman style bathhouse. (Cf. Jer. 36:22.)

All of this tremendous ivory-decorated luxury, which characterized the wealthy and powerful Northern Kingdom when Amos spoke in 760 B.C., was about to cave in within a generation. "A lion has roared! Who will not fear?" (3:8).

10

SUFFERING SHOULD CAUSE REPENTANCE

C. SAMARIA'S FAILURE TO HEED GOD'S CHASTENINGS (4:1-13)

The basic message communicated in chapter 4 of Amos is that God over and over had afflicted the nation of Israel for the primary purpose of causing her people to return to Him in repentance and renewed obedience. This is the lesson summarized in Hebrews 12:5-6, ". . . for those whom the Lord loves He disciplines" (see also Prov. 3:11-12). Five different times in this chapter the Lord recites what He did to Israel to call her back through loving discipline, and each time He sounds the knell, "Yet you have not returned to Me, declares the LORD" (vv. 6, 8, 9, 10, 11).

1. *Your cows will collapse* (4:1-3)

Chapter 3 began with an admonition addressed to the "sons of Israel" (3:1). This term could refer either to the males of Israel or to all the children of that nation, with the context deciding. In 3:1 it appears that the whole nation was addressed. In chapter 4, however, perhaps to balance the mentioning of only the "sons" (and not the daughters) in 3:1, God commences His address by speaking directly to the women "of Samaria" (v. 1).

"Cows of Bashan" refers to the spoiled women of luxury in Samaria. Once understood, it is seen as one of the great metaphors of the Bible. The word *parot* is the feminine plural of *parah*, "cow," whereas the masculine would have been *par*, or plural *parim*, as in Psalm 22:12. Bashan was that land east of the Jordan River that stretched east and southeast for seventy-five miles and was famous for its luxuriant pastures, and hence for its well-fed fat cattle. In Numbers 32:1-5, 16, 26, 33 the tribes of Reuben and Gad (and later half the tribe of Manasseh) asked Moses to grant them the territory of Bashan and Gilead because it appeared so ideal for raising cattle. At the time of Amos, Bashan belonged to the Northern Kingdom. Bashan's heavy milk-producing cows grazing lazily on thick grasses gave the ideal portrait of the luxurious women of Samaria, even though Bashan itself was east of the Jordan River and the city of Samaria was some twenty-five miles west of the Jordan.

The description in verse 1 shows that the women of Samaria oppressed the poor and the needy by making extensive demands on their husbands, which encouraged the husbands to cheat and press more in order to satisfy their wives' demands to drink more.

"The Lord GOD has sworn by His holiness" (v. 2). The title "the Lord GOD" (*Adonai Yehovah*) literally means, "Owner-Master Jehovah." It summons up the name of the ruler of the universe to condemn these queenly tyrants who seem to have no masters or owners (*Adonai*) over them. Verse 1 has shown that it is the women who make the demands upon their husbands. Now it is the Supreme Master, Jehovah, the true owner of all humanity and especially of Israel, who will do the commanding. The name *Jehovah* no doubt also was uttered by the prophet in holy defiance of Baal or the supposed god or gods of the two false altars at Dan and Bethel.

The fact that He swears shows God's absolute determination to bring these women to justice, and that He swears "by His holiness" further emphasizes the holy and righteous nature of God's fearful condemnation. God's holiness—His absolute separation from sin and His righteous requirement that sin be punished—demands Him to judge these sinners.

There is a stern lesson here that should remind us afresh of the power that women have to influence the lives of men, whether for good or for evil.

"Take you away with meat hooks . . . fish hooks" (v. 2). After He follows imagery of heavy, splendid, lazy cows with an oath of certainty, the Lord enunciates the violent fate that awaited the women of Samaria when the Assyrians would invade. The horrible picture of the gashing meat hook, with all its implied tearing and ripping, comes as a sharp contrast to the lazy life of the well bred cow. This portrayed well the savagery of the Assyrian siege, with its breaking down of walls, taking women captive, and dragging them screaming out of their houses. The fishhooks picture a more gentle, baited allurement, but still an action that would end in a violent tug with painful tearing. Perhaps the fishhook describes the later invasions that would eventually empty Samaria and leave it an abandoned, ruined city. The fishhook metaphor, following the meat hook as it does, also fits the view that Sargon II's first invasion in 722-721 B.C. took only about 27,000 of the inhabitants out, whereas later Assyrian monarchs soon completed his damage and finished implementing the policy of moving the population.

"You will go out through breaches" (v. 3). "Breaches" translates the Hebrew word *parotzim,* which refers to an opening or break in a wall. Soon after the June 1967 Six-Day War, when Israel regained Jerusalem for the first time in almost two thousand years, I recall standing amazed as I stared at a huge breach in the Jerusalem wall. It looked so wrong and inappropriate—the gap made the entire city seem naked and open. The Hebrew *parotzim* sounds much like "cows" (*parot,* v. 1), which represented the sinful women of Samaria. The prophet may have purposely had this similarity of sound in mind when he called down judgment upon the sinful women.

The irony is further cast into bold relief when we recall that at the beginning of Israel's history, God made the walls of a city to collapse in great breaches so that His people could enter it as holy judges (Joshua 6:20). Now He calls for breaches so that His people can be dragged out in a similar holy judgment. Joshua 6:20 says of the entrance through the fallen walls of Jericho, "every man [went] straight ahead"; and here in Amos 4:3, "Each one straight before her." In both cases God opens the way for judgment so that at His word it is both direct and swift. This similar language in Joshua and Amos cannot be mere coincidence; it is similar by choice, at the impulse upon the prophet by the Holy Spirit.

The announcement that the women would not leave the city by the ordinary means of going through the gates is a further description of the violent judgment that would befall them. Gaping holes and breaks would be made in the city's walls, and the captives would be led out of those openings nearest to them.

"To Harmon" (v. 3). The women of Samaria were to be taken out and "cast to Harmon." The word *Harmon* is what linguists call a *hapax legomena* (Greek, "once said"), that is, it appears only once in the Bible. The best Hebrew scholars have wrestled over its meaning. Rabbi Rashi translated it "authority"; Hitzig read it as "mountain (*har*) of refuge"; Hesselberg and Maurer as "the high land"; Kimchi and Gesenius as "palace" or "citadel," which the King James Version follows. Another commentator suggests it to be "a woman's apartment"; and Keil says that it is certainly some land or district, but "we have no means of determining it more precisely."[1] The ancient Targums and Symmachus said it was "Armenia."

2. *Your ceremonies will cease* (4:4-5)

Despite the open sin in the land, the people (perhaps here it is still focusing on the women) were zealously making religious pilgrimages to the holy places such as Bethel and Gilgal. Bethel, the place where Jacob dreamed (Gen. 28:10-22), was also the site of one of Jeroboam I's two golden calf altars. Gilgal, the spot of the first Israelite encampment in the promised land, was the place where Samuel judged the nation (1 Sam. 7:16; cf. Josh. 4:19-20).

The words "Enter Bethel and transgress" (v. 4) are an invitation given in irony and biting sarcasm. The coming to the altar of either Bethel or Gilgal, did not please God or put away the sin of those who came. It was rather a further sin against the one true God who established the Temple and altar in Jerusalem (1 Kings 6:1; 8:1).

The English word *transgress* best conveys the idea of sinning "by stepping over a line." But the Hebrew word used here, *pasha'*, primarily signifies "to break a convenant," and it is so used in 2 Kings 1:1.[2] It is the fitting word, because those who came to participate in the false calf-idol worship in Bethel and Gilgal were "breaking God's covenant," namely the second commandment that forbade making or worshiping any idol (Exod. 20:4-5). God declares that despite the people's faithfulness in

---

1. C. F. Keil and F. Delitzsch, *The Twelve Minor Prophets* (Grand Rapids: Eerdmans, n.d.), 1:268-70.
2. William Gesenius, *Hebrew and Chaldee Lexicon*, ed. S. P. Tregelles (Grand Rapids: Eerdmans, 1957), p. 695.

visiting those sacred sites, where God had manifested His presence years before, and despite their offering of sacrifices and tithes there, they were neither pleasing God nor turning from their dual sins of worshiping falsely and oppressing the poor. What good were ceremonies that were not accompanied by repentance and a search after the true God's will? (Cf. Matt. 23: 3-4, 14, 23.) Their zeal to offer, while remaining in a false system, the daily, prescribed sacrifices commanded by Moses (e.g. Num. 28:3-4) is an ailment that still can be observed today among members of zealous but unbiblical cults.

"For so you love to do" (v. 5). God saw in those semi-idolatrous worshipers a love for ceremonial acts. They liked to "do things" rather than to change their hearts, repent, and conform to God's law. How much easier it is even today to perform actions, donate, attend, or bow, then to search our hearts, turn in soul, and then turn in body to follow the Lord.

Misplaced zeal was still Israel's problem in the days of the apostle Paul, as Romans 10:1-3 testifies. Also today one may go to the Wailing Wall in Jerusalem and see the pious Jewish Chasidim (Covenant-Zealots) publicly praying with a zeal such as few in America have ever witnessed. However, such striving for ritual works is not restricted to Israel. People of every race, in every age, have preferred the road of works and ceremonies rather than a quiet voice and heart searching of God's Spirit and Word, which point to repentance and faith in Christ as the only way to God (Rom. 10:4-13).

3. *Your chastisement has called* (4:6-11)

The words repeated five times, "Yet you have not returned to Me," echo again and again in this section. God struck Israel time after time with the rod of divine reproof to turn her away from her sins and back to Him who stood ready to forgive (vv. 6, 8, 9, 10, 11). (See also Matt. 23:37.)

As we consider the means by which God called to Israel during Amos's time, let us keep fresh in our memories that God already had called the nation by the voice of His prophets, the teachings and writings of Moses, and other parts of the Old Testament already written.

The Lord called to Israel by plagues when she would no longer listen to His normal pleas through Moses and "His servants the prophets" (3:7). Note that the Lord also used the for-eign tongues of invaders to get His message across to Israel when His normal method of appealing to her was scorned (Isa. 28:11-12). Paul in 1 Corinthians 14:21-22 uses the Isaiah 28 reference as a proof text that "tongues" are an unusual method to call people who otherwise will not listen to God. So in Amos's day God began to speak to a nonlistening Israel by means of the following things:

Famines and crop failures (v. 6). Here "cleanness of teeth" refers to clean teeth because of a lack of food to eat.

Withholding rain (vv. 7-8). "Three months until harvest" would be at the time of the latter rains, late February through April, at the very time when rain was most needed to produce good crops (Hos. 6:3; Joel 2:23). God also selectively withheld the rain from certain cities. Few things would be as heart searching as having one's fields in a drought while others in the same region were having rain. (See 1 Kings 17:1 when Elijah, at God's bidding, pronounced no rain on the Northern Kingdom a century before Amos.)

"So two or three cities would stagger to another city to drink" (v. 8). With much suffering and inconvenience people would undertake long journeys in their desperation to obtain water, but they would not return in prayer to their God, who was the only one who could restore the rain. They went on journeys, but He was near (Deut. 30:14; John 4:10; James 5:16-18).

Sending natural disasters and pests upon their vineyards and trees (v. 9). Israel shares the same latitudes as the southern third of the United States. In these "horse latitudes" the pre-vailing winds are westerlies, that is, they blow from west to east. For Israel this normally means that moisture collected over the eastern Mediterranean Sea blows eastward and drops in the form of rain before it strikes the Golan and other moun-tains. But according to this verse the winds had reversed, and the dry, hot desert winds from the east had tended to absorb whatever moisture was in the area over Israel. That process had dried out the land and its crops. God controlled the winds, but Israel did not return to Him.

Yereq in Hebrew means "green," but here Amos uses *yarek-on*, "green-ish," and it refers to the *pale green* color of a dis-eased or mildewed plant. Mildew is a discoloration caused by fungus. This was combined with the caterpillar, which might have been a wingless locust (Hebrew *gazam*, a "cutting-off insect"; see Joel 1:4 and 2:25). The point is, their gardens and trees did not grow because of the drought, *but* if something did grow, the mildew got it. If it somehow also escaped the mildew, the insects came along and devoured it. I have personally felt the joy of thrilling to beautiful fruit trees on one morning and the pain of crying the next, as Japanese beetles devoured the leaves of entire trees in one day. It is so desperately discouraging. One cannot imagine it unless he has experienced it. That kind of judgment should have driven the Israelites to their knees in repentance and prayer, but it did not. Amos is affirming that the plagues of Deuteronomy 28:22, 39-40, 42 were coming to pass.

Allowing plagues and battle defeats to bring death (v. 10). Exodus 8:22 and 9:26 record that God had smitten Egypt with plagues, but in both instances He had spared the land of Goshen where the Hebrews lived at the time. Now that is reversed. God is smiting Israel with those plagues that He previously had reserved only for idolators and enemies who hardened their hearts toward Him. Likewise the book of Joshua indicates that, except for the incident in Joshua 7:5 in which thirty-six Israelites were lost at Ai because of sin in the camp, God had shielded His people during times of battle. Now that principle also is reversed, and He is supernaturally intervening to defeat Israel in battle. This too should have brought the people to their knees both collectively and individually, but, in accord with the statement of Matthew 23:37, they would not come. There is a lesson for today's America, and for all nations, in these verses.

"The stench of your camp" refers to the smell of the dead bodies after a defeat in battle (cf. Isa. 34:3).

By nearly destroying the nation (v. 11). The destruction described was probably the successive defeats of the Northern Kingdom by the Syrians under Hazael. The defeats were against Jehoram (841 B.C., 2 Kings 8:28-29); Jehu (820 B.C., 2 Kings 10:32-33); and Jehoahaz (810 B.C., 2 Kings 13:3-7, 22).[3] The victories that God gave Jeroboam II in order to save Israel dur-

3. John H. Walton, *Chronological Charts of the Old Testament* (Grand Rapids: Zondervan, 1978), pp. 62-63.

ing Amos's day are described in 2 Kings 14:23-27. "The LORD did not say that He would blot out the name of Israel" (v. 27). This is precisely the meaning of the words here, "a firebrand snatched from a blaze," that is, "the phrase is proverbial for a narrow escape from utter extinction."[4]

4. *Your Creator is coming* (4:12-13)

"Therefore . . . prepare to meet your God, O Israel" (v. 12). The word *laken* expresses causality and is well translated by "therefore" or "on account of." Here we are told that *because* Israel had not turned back to the Lord, despite the callings of the prophets and the smitings of the plagues just named, *therefore* she should prepare to meet her God, not just another prophet whom she might choose to ignore.

"The LORD God of hosts is His name" (v. 13). This chapter concludes with a description of the One with whom those spurners of mercy finally will have to deal. He is the creator of the earth, of its mountains, and of the winds that can blow men on ships and on camel caravans off their courses. He is not merely some mortal prophet like Amos, whom Jeroboam II may ignore and whom the people may jeer at. God is also not like a righteous human being who can be fooled by pious nods followed by no repentance or change of life. He is the God who can read man's thoughts. Yes, He who controls the world and whose presence is everywhere is about to deal personally with this nation that is too rich, too preoccupied, and too callous to listen to the prophets.

After the preceding powerful description of the Lord to a nation that had repeatedly ignored His rod of anger, the prophet concludes with naming Him as the one whom it is impossible to ignore—"the LORD God of hosts." In the Old Testament the title "LORD of hosts" is applied 282 times to God.[5] It pictures God as the leader both of the Israelite army (1 Sam. 17:45) and of the countless and powerful unseen spiritual forces standing at His disposal (Josh. 5:13-14). This title is equivalent to a triumphant announcement, designed to put fear into its hearers,

---

4. Robert Jamieson, A. R. Fausset, and David Brown, *Commentary on the Whole Bible* (Grand Rapids: Zondervan, 1962), p. 794.
5. W. Clow, *Bible Reader's Encyclopedia and Concordance,* rev. ed. (New York: Collins, 1977), p. 236.

that Israel's coming foe would be none other than the "God of Battle," namely, "the LORD of hosts." The addition of *God* (*Elohim*) here serves even further to magnify the title. This is much like Revelation 19:11, 16, in which at His second coming Christ appears to destroy the Antichrist and his armies with the title written upon His thigh, "KING OF KINGS, AND LORD OF LORDS."

Note: It is of interest that the modern name for the Israeli army is Israeli Defense Force. In Hebrew this is known officially as TZAHAL, an acronym formed by the initial letters of *Tzavaot Haganah le-Yisrael*, "The-Host-of Defense for-Israel." As in Amos 4:13 and throughout the Old Testament, the expression *the hosts* means "the armies." Luther so used it in the second stanza of his battle hymn "A Mighty Fortress Is Our God," in which we sing, *"Lord Sab-a-oth* [of hosts] his name,/From age to age the same,/And he must win the battle (italics added)." Accordingly, Amos's announcement that Israel was about to face "the LORD God of hosts" meant that God had at last declared war on that sinful nation.

May we also learn the lesson of this chapter and see the danger of ignoring God's gentle entreaties by His Spirit through His word, lest we have to face Him as the "LORD God of Hosts" who has declared war on us. This lesson surely applies to individuals as well as to nations.

11

CEREMONIES WILL NOT SAVE THE UNREPENTANT

D. SAMARIA'S FALSE RELIGION CONDEMNED (5:1-27)

1. *God's dirge for Israel* (5:1-3)

"Hear this word . . . a dirge" (v. 1). The tone of chapter 5 is set by the word *dirge*. In Hebrew it is *qinah*, "a mournful song, a lamentation." The word comes from the root *qin*, "to strike a musical instrument." The King James Version translates it here as "lamentation." The related Arab word is *qayna*, which means "a female minstrel or any female singer."[1]

Thus, the prophet tells all his hearers that he has bad news for the nation Israel: a song of lamentation, befitting a nation that is about to die, or that is perhaps already dead.

"She has fallen, she will not rise again—the virgin Israel (v. 2). The prophet begins his song of lamentation. Israel is called, in today's language, "a fallen woman." The word for *virgin* is *betulah* and refers to a "pure and unspotted" woman. Amos sees the nation either as fallen into sin or as fallen to the ground from her former erect posture. He adds the awful pronouncement that "she will not rise again." Israel evidently did not rise again through moral repentance, because God did not spare her as He offered to do if she would but turn to Him (vv. 4, 6, 14). After Samaria fell to the Assyrians in 722 B.C. she never arose to be a nation again. Even in the Millennial age, after the Lord's second coming, the Northern Kingdom still will not be restored as a separate nation. At that time, both she and Judah shall be united into one new Israel (see Ezek. 37:15-28).

"There is none to raise her up" (v. 2). Of course, only God could raise her up, but He was the very One who was putting

1. William Gesenius, *Hebrew and Chaldee Lexicon*, ed. S. P. Tregelles (Grand Rapids: Eerdmans, 1957), pp. 728-29, 731.

her down because of her sins. It was the same in 586 B.C. when the Babylonians destroyed Jerusalem and Solomon's Temple and again in A.D. 70 when the Romans crushed Jerusalem and the second Temple. In those cases also, only God could have saved, but it was He who judged.

"A thousand . . . a hundred left" (v. 3). This prophetic dirge would come to pass literally, as the Assyrians would press their policy of population manipulation and eventually would force the exodus of most Israelites out of the land.

2. *God's directions to Israel* (5:4-7)

"Seek Me that you may live" (v. 4). The word *seek* is *darash,* meaning "to seek, to search after, to apply oneself to study or follow someone or something."[2] From this word comes *midarash,* "seeking," which in Judaism refers to the study of the sacred texts of the Torah (biblical law) and the Talmud (rabbinical learning). Therefore, the prophet points the nation to the supreme truth that her following the true God and seeking after His presence, laws, and true worship was the one way she still could preserve her national spiritual life. This ultimate truth is reiterated in verses 6 and 14, and in principle in countless other Bible verses (e.g. John 10:7, 9).

"But do not resort to Bethel" (v. 5). The Hebrew word that is translated "seek" in verse 4 is translated "resort" in this verse. The cities of Bethel, Gilgal, and Beersheba each had been sacred at one time in Israel's history; but now, because of the false religion and oppression found in those places, each had fallen to abominations. The destiny of those places, and the implied fate of persons who resorted there, would be "captivity" and "trouble" (v. 5); whereas those who sought the Lord would have a destiny of "life" (v. 4).

"O house of Joseph . . . those who turn justice into wormwood" (vv. 6-7). Here "the house of Joseph" is addressed, and this is another title for the Northern Kingdom. Joseph's two sons were Ephraim and Manasseh, from whom sprang two tribes that became the two strongest among the ten tribes of the Northern Kingdom. Therefore those names together, and sometimes merely Ephraim alone, are synonymous with the Northern Kingdom (e.g. Isa. 7:2).

2. Ibid., p. 209.

The nation's crime was so great in God's sight that He portrays it as one who perverts justice into "wormwood" (*la-enah*), a bitter tasting and poisonous root (Deut. 29:18; Jer. 9:15; Rev. 8:11). Those who lit sacrificial fire to the calves at Bethel would soon discover they had ignited a fire of punishment that would burn them with judgment. Ultimately, such a fire will never go out. (See Mark 9:48.)

"And cast righteousness down to the earth" (v. 7). Here the causative form of *nu-ach* ("to rest, sit down") is translated, "cast."[3] In Exodus 33:14 it is translated, "I will give you rest [from the Canaanites]." The emphasis of the Hebrew is that righteousness has been put to rest on the ground, laid aside, and forgotten—not that it has been thrown away or cast down. The sinful society of Samaria is now amoral, no longer even concerned with a righteous standard that has been laid to rest someplace where it will disturb no one.

3. *God's deity over Israel* (5:8-9)

The previous warnings exhorted the people not to "resort to Bethel" or the other sites of false religion. Now Amos gives a resounding affirmation of the name and power of the true God, whom he holds up in stark opposition to the helpless calf god of wood and gold.

"The LORD is His name" (v. 8). The LORD in Hebrew is the sacred "Tetragram," the four letters YHWH. Centuries of Bible scribes considered that name too sacred to be pronounced. Thus, its exact pronunciation is uncertain and disputed. Some have thought it to be *Jehovah*, but the majority today favor *Yaweh*. It might be a name that only those in heaven know the meaning of. It appears probable, however, to be the verb form *he is*. If so, it is a name that affirms the eternal existence and character of God. Amos's use of this name here, compared with the dead, lifeless, and temporary images upon the altars of the Northern Kingdom, is most appropriate.

"He who made the Pleiades" (v. 8). With the affirmation of the name of the true God, Amos adds an equal affirmation of His powers as creator and sustainer of the universe. It is He who formed the star constellations in the heavens (cf. Job 9:9)

3. Ibid., pp. 538-39.

and who causes the daily rotation of the earth, which gives night and morning. God is the one who sends the rains that grow crops, which feed the earth (v. 8). The clear implication is that He is therefore the only one to whom Israel ought to pray—not to golden calves, even if such idols are backed by Jeroboam II himself. The Pleiades is that beautiful star cluster in the constellation Taurus (the Bull), the seven brightest stars that can be seen with the naked eye. Orion is the chief constellation of the winter sky. These wondrous objects in the sky show the true God's glory and power (Psalm 19:1).

"Who flashes forth with destruction" (v. 9). The verb *balag* is translated "flashes," which in this context means "to cause to shine forth (like the dawn)."[4] The prophet now adds a note of judgment. This powerful God of creation is also the One who can bring sudden destruction. He can vanquish both the strong person and army, as well as the mighty man-made fortress. The argument here is that the power of the Lord ought to make us fear Him and serve Him. It is a lesson as valid today as it was twenty-seven centuries ago. (See Deut. 10:12; Josh. 4:24; Matt. 10:28.)

4. *God's dismay over Israel* (5:10-13)

"They hate him who reproves in the gate" (v. 10). Those who do evil in this world do not always passively hang their heads in shame when they are confronted with their sins. In the same way, in Amos's day some persons snarled back with hatred at anyone who sought to rebuke or correct them. Because its root meaning is "to be straight" (in front of someone),[5] the word *reproves* (*yakach*) teaches its own lesson. In ancient times the town elders often sat at the city gates to rebuke open sinners who entered or exited the city. In Amos's day apparently he and the elders did this kind of rebuking. They received hatred for it. The people should have been struck in their consciences and should have turned to God in true repentance. Perhaps that rebuking took place in the gates of Bethel, where many were entering to worship at the calf altar. (Cf. Matt. 5:12; Luke 6:22; 21:17.)

Verse 13 is discussed next because it complements verse 10.

4. Ibid., p. 121.
5. Ibid., pp. 347, 550.

"Therefore, at such a time the prudent person keeps silent" (v. 13). There arrive moments when all that can be said has been said and the issues are clear. Then, if the one rebuked has firmly decided not to listen and turns in hatred or violence toward the one who would see him converted, further argument is futile and physically dangerous. That was the case in Samaria, and frail righteous people knew to hold their tongues. (Cf. Matt. 7:6; Luke 23:9; John 19:9-10.)

Judgments that fit the crime are seen in verse 11. Those who cheat the poor by charging an inflated rent will in turn be put out of their own homes, which were made beautiful and strong by the revenues of wickedness. Those who place upon the poor extra and unnecessary charges in the buying and selling of grain will in turn have their own farm products taxed away by God. And the farms and food that the wicked will lose ("pleasant vineyards . . . wine") are more elaborate than those of the poor whom they rob.

"You . . . accept bribes, and turn aside the poor in the gate" (v. 12). The righteous who are left in Samaria are "distressed," especially when they see justice openly perverted, both in minor cases "in the gate" and in major trials in court hearings. The wicked, who have money to influence the judges, are either not put on trial or are set free. The poor, who have no money to give as bribes or who would not do such a thing, are sent away and informed that the elders and courts have too busy a docket even to hear their trivial cases. God says that those "sins are great." Such actions were explicitly forbidden earlier in the the Old Testament (Exod. 23:6-9; Num. 35:31; Deut. 16:18-20).

5. *God's demands for Israel* (5:14-15)

"Seek good and not evil, that you may live" (v. 14). Here the invitation is given again to Israel to change her entire manner of life, to have righteousness as her new goal. The reward for such a change would be life—national preservation, individual survival, and eternal spiritual life. Such a turn around can come about only by a new faith in the one true God, a *born again* experience such as Christ later would describe in John 3:3. In Samaria people were much like they are today. One can plead with the sinner and show him what his awful life is doing to himself and those around him, but all such sessions can be futile. One has to be reborn from above in order to turn from evil toward a thirsting after righteousness.

"Perhaps the LORD God of hosts may be gracious" (v. 15). Judgment has already been pronounced against the Northern Kingdom (2:6; 5:3), yet at the same time the prophet holds out a hand of mercy. The "perhaps" is given with the hope that the Lord will look with favor upon a late repentance and commute the sentence. The classic cases of this are: Ahab, 1 Kings 21:20-29; Hezekiah, Isaiah 38:1-5; and Levi, who was to have his tribe scattered for his sin with Simeon, Genesis 34:25-31; 49:5-7. God made that scattering a blessing by assigning to the Levites the holy ministrations in the Tabernacle and Temple and throughout Israel (Num. 7:5; Josh. 21). Moses, Aaron, and all the priesthood were Levites. This fact surely ought to give hope even to the judged, as long as there is life and the working of the Spirit.

"To the remnant of Joseph" (v. 15). Sixty years before, in 820 B.C., Hazael of Syria had conquered much of the Northern Kingdom. Therefore, those that survived in Amos's day could still be called a "remnant" (*sha-ar*, "remaining ones"), despite the temporary resurgence of national strength then being manifested.

Amos is placing before the nation the choice of God's having mercy upon the children of the survivors of past judgments, or of God's completing the demise of the Northern Kingdom. The prophet tells the people of the judgments that will come if they continue in sin, and then he urges them to the path of repentance, life, and mercy.

6. *God's drawing near to Israel* (5:16-20)

Those Who Wail at It (vv. 16-17). Here the speaker is "the LORD [*Jehovah*] God of hosts, the Lord [*Adonai*, "master"]. Jamieson calls this "an accumulation of titles, of which His lordship over all things is the climax, to mark that from His judgment there is no appeal."[6] The prophet now looks ahead by the Spirit of prophecy and sees the destruction of Samaria by the Assyrians and the awful scenes of weeping and wailing that will soon come upon this stubborn and unhearing people. The word

6. Robert Jamieson, A. R. Fausset, and David Brown, *Commentary on the Whole Bible* (Grand Rapids: Zondervan, 1962), p. 796.

for "wailing" is *misfad,* the gerund of the verb *safad,* "to beat the breast as a sign of grief, especially for the dead."[7] So, this nation that hates the prophet's cries at the city gates against its sins, verse 10, will soon be giving forth its own cries of anguish in the streets.

Those Who Long for It (vv. 18-20). From these verses it is evident that some in Samaria were "longing for the day of the LORD" (v. 18). Jamieson believes Amos is here replying to cynics who had ridiculed him. Ironically, they had done so by mocking that they were anxious for the Lord to come and visit them. Amos then pronounces woe on the cynics by taking up their taunting words as if they had meant them.[8]

Keil seems to have a better explanation, namely, that many in Israel knew the prophecy of Joel 3, which had spoken sixty years before of the Lord's coming to deliver Judah and Israel and to judge the nations that oppressed them.[9] They looked upon God, much as Israel did in Jesus' time, as the one who would deliver the Jews automatically, as a racial right. They forgot the concomitant requirement that those who wished to be delivered had to call upon the Lord in repentance (Joel 2: 32).

"It will be darkness and not light" (v. 18). Israel rightly thought that were God to come, He would defeat the sinful Gentiles; but Amos announces that God also would destroy the sinful works of Samaria. It would go badly for Samaria on the day that God arrived for judgment. The judgment messages of chapters 1 and 2 show us this truth. There God does judge six wicked Gentile nations, but He also judges Judah and Israel for their sins. The sinners of Samaria did not wish to consider a judgment of themselves. In every generation the wicked have eyes blinded to the light of truth and refuse to look at it. (See Matt. 7:1-5.)

Note: "The day of the LORD" refers to any period when the Lord enters into human affairs and judges. It is a supernatural or providential intervention, in which God usually uses secondary causes and means (men, kings, armies, and nature).

7. Gesenius, pp. 490, 592.
8. Jamieson, Fausset, and Brown, p. 796.
9. C. F. Keil and F. Delitzsch, *The Twelve Minor Prophets* (Grand Rapids: Eerdmans, n.d.), 1:287.

Sometimes it refers to the end of the age and to those events connected with the second coming of Christ and its aftermath (1 Thess. 5:1-3; 2 Pet. 3:10-12). At other times, such as here in verse 18, "the day of the LORD" refers to a limited, historical judgment of a sinful people.

Surely the pictures of a man meeting one awful animal after another, painted by Amos in verses 19 and 20, were accurate pictures of the evils that would fall successively upon the people of the Northern Kingdom at the hands of Assyria, Babylon, Syria, Rome, the Ottoman Turks, and present-day enemies.

7. *God's denial of Israel* (5:21-26)

"I hate, I reject your festivals" (vv. 21-23). What God lashes out against here is: (a) Israel's *false worship* with the golden calves upon the altars at Bethel and Dan, and (b) *worship not accompanied by faith and works.* The mere performance of ceremonies will not save the unrepentant.

Sacerdotalism is the doctrine that ceremonies themselves can grant righteousness to the one who participates in them. Close to this was the idea of the twelfth and thirteenth centuries that God would justify a person merely because he went on one of the Crusades; faith and repentance were not factors. That is false religion, and God makes clear that He will not be swayed by it. Thus Paul says that true faith is necessary for salvation (Rom. 4:1-9), and James adds that true faith must show its living quality by producing at least a measure of good works (James 2:17). To this we must add Amos's claim that ceremonies alone—and wrong ceremonies at that—save no one.

Some, notably unbelievers and liberals who reject the inspiration of the Scriptures, lift this section of Amos out of context and use it to claim that God was never desirous of all the ceremonies and offerings that the Old Testament commands. They look upon the entire sacrificial system as an invention of "priestcraft." Consequently, this part of Amos is represented as the high-water mark of Old Testament ethical and religious thought. The prophet at last sees that it is goodness, fair play, and kindness that make up true religion. The sacrificial system is simply a human invention by the priests to keep the people in line. All this is the argument of unbelievers.

This line of reasoning is contrary to biblical revelation, because it was God who established a worship ceremony by which a sinful people could approach Him on the substitute merit of animal blood. That system foreshadowed the substitutionary death of the Messiah (Heb. 9:12).

"But let justice roll down like waters" (v. 24). Here Amos calls both the nation and the individual to a complete turn around in life-style, a conversion experience. Where there is no justice, only oppression, the entire picture must be reversed, and righteousness must be allowed to flow strongly and continually. This verse does not ask for mere improvement, better effort, or a little more justice and a bit less sin. Rather, it asks for a conversion that completely stops injustice and sin and opens the dam to let righteous worship, true belief, and proper treatment of others flow in fullness and power. Only a true conversion would suspend God's sentence against the Northern Kingdom. This message was what made Amos a true prophet of last warning.

"In the wilderness for forty years . . . Sikkuth . . . Kiyyun, your images, the star" (vv. 25-26). Here the argument is that the Israelites of the Northern Kingdom were repeating the same sins that had been characteristic of that rebellious generation in the wilderness. While those people had worshiped God at the Tabernacle, they had also secretly worshiped the pagan images they had brought along from Egypt. That comparison aptly fits the Northern Kingdom's confusion of worshiping the true God *and* the calf images at Bethel and Dan (1 Kings 12: 28-29).

The words *sikkuth* and *kiyyun* occur only here, and therefore it is not certain what the translations should be. Keil, one of the all-time great Hebrew scholars, suggests, "But have ye borne the *booth (sikkuth)* of your *king (molech)* and the *pedestal (kiyyun)* of your images . . .?"[10] The message is clear. Israel was mixing oppression and the breaking of God's law with a worship that blended a large cup of paganism with the true worship of the Lord. God would not accept this kind of religion. He did not accept it in the forty years of wilderness wanderings, and He would not accept it from Samaria in Amos's day. Will He accept

10. Ibid., 1:289-92.

it any more today? Surely this is also a clear lesson for us. (See 1 Cor. 10:5-7, 21.)

8. *God's decision for Israel* (5:27)

"Therefore, I will make you go into exile beyond Damascus" (v. 27). In Acts 7:42-43 Stephen paraphrased Amos 5:25-27 and concluded with, "I ALSO WILL REMOVE YOU BEYOND BABYLON." Stephen purposely said Babylon instead of Damascus because he was speaking after the Northern Kingdom had been scattered beyond Damascus by the Assyrians in 721 B.C., and after Judah had been carried beyond Babylon in 586 B.C. by the Babylonians. That both instances were perfectly fulfilled is beyond question. Eventually the people of Samaria were driven not only beyond nearby Damascus but also beyond Babylon to the far corners of the globe. Those who would not yield themselves to the protection of the true God found themselves captured by the wicked of this world, and the rejected "God of hosts" allowed it to happen in His righteous judgment.

12

CONFIDENCE WILL NOT SAVE
THE UNREPENTANT

E. SAMARIA'S EASE TO BE TURNED TO SUFFERING (6:1-14)

1. *God's message to those at ease in Zion—calamity coming* (6:1-3).

"Woe to those . . . at ease in Zion" (v. 1). *Hoi* is the Hebrew word of admonition and lamentation, much like our English *woe*. Amos directs that word at those who were "at ease" (*shaanan*, "resting quietly"), and those who were "secure" (*batach*, "trusting in"). The trust that provided those sinners their security was "the mountain of Samaria" (v. 1). Instead of finding their security in the Lord, they were trusting in the strength of Samaria, a city built upon a strong defensible hill, and in all the armed might under the hand of Jeroboam II. The verse goes on to mention that important foreigners came and went amid this great metropolis. It exuded confidence.

"Go over to Calneh and look . . . Hamath . . . Gath" (v. 2). Calneh was a Babylonian and Assyrian capital city, filled with temples, on the east bank of the Tigris River. Hamath was the capital of a Syrian state of the same name, and it was on the banks of the Orontes River. Gath was one of the five capitals of the Philistines, which by this time had lost its former grandeur.[1] All three cities had at one time been great, and all had now fallen into decay. Thus, Amos tells those who rest in Samaria's strength that they should look at the record of history, at similar cities and nations of the past who neglected or rejected God.

"Do you put off the day of calamity, and . . . bring near the seat of violence?" (v. 3). Here the prophet points with irony at

---

1. I offer the above explanation for Calneh notwithstanding that almost every other book locates the city at a different place and paints it in a different condition.

the people's contrasting actions. They "push away" (*nadah*) their day of reckoning with the Lord, while still "pulling close" (*nagash*) their sinful, violent lives. On the one hand he asks them sarcastically if they think they really can "put off the day of calamity (*yom ra*, "day of evil")." The verbal form *put off* is *nadah*, and it means "to remove or cast out someone or something." In the Talmud, the writings that record the words of the ancient rabbis, this word is used to designate the excommunication of someone from the synagogue congregation.[2] So Amos seems to be saying, "Do you think you can eliminate God's coming day of judgment by excommunicating it from your lives and thoughts?"

Next, in a purposeful contrast to *nadah,* the prophet asks, "And would you bring near the seat of violence?" Here, in the second half of the verse, "bring near" (*nagash*) is in direct contrast to "put away" in the first half. Simply put, he is asking, "How can you *push away* God's judgment when you *pull close* to yourselves sinful violence?" *Chamas,* "violence," refers to sinful oppression.[3] Amos tells them that such thinking is a contradiction—you cannot live in sinful violence and at the same time expect God to be at peace with you. Therefore, God's message to those at ease in Zion is, "Your calamity is coming!"

2. God's message to those in luxury in Samaria—exile coming (6:4-7)

"Those who recline on beds of ivory" (vv. 4-6). Until J. W. Crowfoot excavated Samaria in 1931, many scholars suggested that Amos's portrait in these verses of the decadent luxury of Samaria was merely figurative. The 1931 excavation changed all such thinking. Ivory plaques, sculptured panels, inlaid pieces, and furniture dowels were found with bas-reliefs upon them of "lotus, lilies, papyrus, lions, bulls, deer, winged figures in human form, sphinxes, and figures of Egyptian gods, such as Isis and Horus."[4] Such a discovery documented not only Samaria's luxury, but also its religious laxity, which pervaded the city and apparently allowed the sewers of moral corruption to flow freely.

2. William Gesenius, *Hebrew and Chaldee Lexicon,* ed. S. P. Tregelles (Grand Rapids: Eerdmans, 1957), p. 534.
3. Ibid., p. 288.
4. Joseph P. Free, *Archeology and Bible History* (Wheaton, Ill.: Scripture Press, 1956), pp. 193-94.

Verses 4-6 paint what to many is the "good life"—good food, plenty of drink, the finest glasses, beautiful furniture, music, and money enough to allow plenty of time for lounging in wantonness. (See also Luke 12:15, 16-21; 1 John 2:15.)

"Who drink wine from sacrificial bowls" (v. 6). The sinners of Samaria indeed possess "sacrificial bowls." The word so translated (*mizraki*) refers to the holy "basins" of the altar (Exodus 38:3). However, instead of using such sacred utensils as part of a true worship—containing the blood to be sprinkled—which leads to genuine repentance, those of Samaria here are using those vessels as part of their drunken celebrations. Likewise their "finest of oils" are not those used to anoint people to God's service (Lev. 8:12), but rather those used for a simple rubdown to make one more relaxed.

"Yet they have not grieved over the ruin of Joseph" (v. 6). This luxurious living amid basins and oils was not complemented with spiritual beauty. There was no grieving for sin here, no personal repentance, no asking God for forgiveness and strength to live for Him, and no weeping or prayer for the nation, which was daily sinking deeper into sin.

"Therefore, they will now go into exile at the head of the exiles" (v. 7). Those who spurn God often discover that His divine justice prevents Him from moving to help them when their calamity comes. God could have delivered the Northern Kingdom from the Assyrians, just as He had delivered Israel so many times before with His mighty hand. This nation, however, wanted to block itself off from the knowledge and covenant of the true God. The Egyptian gods Isis and Horus, would not lift a wing to help the people. The sinners in Samaria led the nation into sin and rebellion; now they would cause the nation to be led into exile at the hand of Assyria's Shalmaneser V and Sargon II. This would at last halt the nation's sinful partying. Amos's message must have been all the more biting because it no doubt came from a man who, by his prophetic garb and severity of manner, portrayed an austere life so opposite from that of his party-going listeners.

Banquets and suppers in themselves are not evil; apparently Jesus often attended such social occasions. However, sinful parties, which make a mockery of God, are those that Amos portrays here. (Cf. Esther 1:1-12; Isa. 28:1-3; Dan. 5.)

3. *God's message to those in arrogance—lowliness coming* (6:8-11)

"I loathe the arrogance of Jacob" (v. 8). First with an oath upon His sacred name, and then with the mention of His name of war, "The LORD God of hosts," God pronounces in verse 8 His absolute abhorrence (*ta-av*, "to hate, abhor") upon the Northern Kingdom's "arrogance" (*gaon*, "exaltation"). The Hebrew structure gives the thought even more power, "*I loathe* the arrogance of Jacob, and his citadels *I hate!*" It begins and ends the pronouncement with words of hatred, *ta-av*, "to loathe," and *sane*, "to hate."

Let anyone reading these words consider the appropriateness or inappropriateness of this hypothetical scene: Amos's driving about in Samaria in a chariot with a twentieth-century-style bumper sticker on its rear reading, "Smile, God Loves You!" Yes, God "loves you" enough to have sent Christ to die for you and loves you enough to call you to repentance and faith. However, I have heard with my own ears a liberal explain that God *approves and accepts* everyone just as he is. This surely is not Amos's message to a sinful generation (cf. Phil. 2:15).

"If ten men are left in one house, they will die" (vv. 9-11). These three verses paint a masterful picture of a nation and people brought to the very depths of humility. God, the master-painter of lives and history, is at work in Samaria, changing the canvas into one that would match His holy demands. The death toll and destruction that would be brought by the waves of Assyrian marauders would leave no room for cheerful or hopeful speech, even if it were religious. The point of verse 9 is that God's coming judgment against Samaria will be so unrelenting that even if the inhabitants of a large house should be fortunate enough to survive the invaders, death by pestilence will ultimately slay them.

"The name of the LORD is not to be mentioned" (v. 10). Here the scene is one of relatives gathering bodies for burial amid God's allowing the Assyrian attackers to destroy the nation. At such a time it would be more than ever normal and proper for the name of God to be evoked continuously over the dead. Instead, here we find the use of God's name being forbidden. Why, we must ask, did some of the people here forbid others to mention the name of the Lord? Was it because of a realization that they had sinned so greatly and were no longer fit to mention so holy a name? Or was it done in bitterness against the Lord because they were blaming Him for the judgment that had overtaken them? Or were they blaming Him for not helping them in their hour of need? Jamieson suggests that the person carrying the bodies outside was admonishing the lone survivor inside not to praise the Lord for his own survival because, amid the carnage, such praise would be inappropriate.[5] Ryrie suggests that the speaker feared the mere mention of the Lord's name here would bring on more judgment.[6]

It should be noted that the word *undertaker* in v. 10 is *miseraph*, literally "a burner," hence the diseases, and perhaps the large number of dead, required cremation rather than the usual Hebrew custom of burial—except in the case of the badly mutilated or criminals (Josh. 7:25; 1 Sam. 31:12).

4. *God's message to those confident in Israel—affliction coming* (6:12-14)

"Do horses run on rocks?" (v. 12). With this metaphor and the one that follows ("or does one plow them with oxen?"), God attempts to show Israel the futility of two inequalities the people still held in their minds. First, He sought to show them that their perversion of justice in their courts *would not equal* the righteousness of God's standards. He saw their actions as "poison" and "wormwood." Second, the military might of Jeroboam II, *would not equal* the might of the Assyrian bands that God would pit against Israel (v. 13). So God declares that the people's confidence is illogical and in vain.

"You who rejoice in Lo-debar" (v. 13). *Lo-debar* is two Hebrew words that are the idiom for *nothing*. Even in modern Hebrew one says *lo-debar* when he wants to say, "It's nothing; it doesn't matter; forget it." Literally, the words mean, "no (*lo*) word (*debar*)." Here God calls Israel's confident rejoicing in the momentary upsurge of her strength under Jeroboam II *lo debar*, "nothing," in His sight. Israel was boasting in Jeroboam II's recent conquests of the nearby local areas and confidently saying that she had taken up the *Karnaim*, the "horns"

---

5. Robert Jamieson, A. R. Fausset, and David Brown, *Commentary on the Whole Bible* (Grand Rapids: Zondervan, 1962), p. 747.
6. Charles C. Ryrie, *The Ryrie Study Bible* (Chicago: Moody, 1978), p. 1366.

of military conquest. The horns of animals were the animals' glory as well as their weapons for fighting.[7] Israel was proud of her military might and was not afraid. She was thinking of offensive conquests, not any destruction such as gloomy Amos seemed to be so unrealistically proclaiming. (Cf. Psalm 75:10; Lam. 2:3, 17; Mic. 4:13.)

"They will afflict you from the entrance of Hamath to the brook of the Arabah" (v. 14). Here *afflict* is *lachatz,* "to press, squeeze." The same word is used of Balaam's donkey being *squeezed* against the wall (Num. 22:25) and a man being *pushed* outside against the door (2 Kings 6:32). God is about to push and squeeze Israel out of Samaria.[8]

Hamath (see also 6:2) marked one of the northern boundaries of Israel, and Jeroboam II had recently repossessed it. It would be through here that the Assyrians would invade Israel from the north.

Scholars have debated the location of the brook of the Arabah. The Arabah is the dry southland desert between the Dead Sea and the Gulf of Eilat (Aqaba). This brook has been named as the *Kidron,* which after a strong rain occasionally flows into the valley east of Jerusalem (Jamieson); and as the *Nile* (Grotius). From the context the stream is most probably some river or wadi that marked the south end of the Northern Kingdom's newly enlarged territory. So the Lord is telling the Israelites that His might is greater than theirs, and that He was about to subjugate all the land they owned. If Grotius is correct, and the brook of the Arabah refers to the Nile or even to any water body in the south of Israel, then the meaning could be that the Assyrians would chase the Israelites not only out of Samaria, but also into southern Palestine, far beyond the Northern Kingdom's borders. (See 1 Kings 8:65.)

Chapter 6 is replete with lessons concerning the futility of misplaced confidence. The vain trust portrayed here is in sharp contrast to the gentle, sure offer that Christ holds out to sinners, as in Matthew 11:28-30.

---

7. In many prophetic sections, horns represent kings (Dan. 7:24; Rev. 17:12). Here, however, they represent offensive military might.
8. Gesenius, p. 437.

13

CHASING THE PREACHER WILL NOT SAVE THE UNREPENTANT

V. Amos's Visions of Coming Judgment (7:1–9:15)

A. vision of the locust swarm (7:1-3)

In the remaining chapters God shows Amos six visions, five of which unite in showing the destruction of the Northern Kingdom (7:1-3; 7:4-6; 7:7-9; 8:1-3; 9:1-4—but 9:11-15 shows future blessings). In this first vision God is seen assembling a swarm of locusts. The Hebrew *gov* (pronounced like *stove*) refers to the large grasshopper or locust of Israel. The word is from the verb *govah*, "to come forth from the earth," and hence the multiplied thousands and even millions of locusts that appeared in a plague seemed to spring right out of the earth (cf. Exod. 10:4; Deut. 28:38; Psalm 105:34; Prov. 30:27; Nah. 3:17; Rev. 9:3, 7). It has been said of the locust, "These voracious insects are migratory, and often appear in huge darkening swarms, settling on and devouring every green thing and leaving barrenness behind. They are still prized for food, Lev 11:22; Mt 3:4."[1]

"The spring crop" (v. 1). The Hebrew *lekesh* refers to the spring harvests of barley (March-April) and wheat (April-June). These follow the spring or latter rains of March and April, known as the *malqosh*. The early rains fall from the close of November and continue through January, softening the baked summer ground. The more important latter rains of the spring, however, provide the water necessary for the growth of the crop.

Here in Amos 7 the locusts attacked just as the crop began to grow. In so doing, they threatened to wipe out everything. The

---

1. W. Clow, *Bible Reader's Encyclopedia and Concordance,* rev. ed. (New York: Collins, 1977), p. 235.

words "after the king's mowing" are a puzzle. *Gaz,* the word used here for *mowing* means the shearing of sheep or the cutting down of grass, as used in Psalm 72:6. Keil suggests that God is the king who has already mowed, or punished, Israel by various judgments.[2] The more probable explanation is simply that the king required an early mowing for a tax, a firstfruits of the hay crop, so that the large number of royal cattle and horses could now be fed well again.[3] If that's true, the locust plague would occur at a crucial moment, when the farmers' winter supplies would be exhausted, and when they could barely wait any longer to have new grass to feed their waiting animals. The picture of the locusts eating the crops is therefore a representation of how God would destroy the ten tribes.

Amos, like Moses before him in Numbers 14:11-21, interceded for Israel, and the Lord held back and did not utterly destroy the people of the Northern Kingdom. The eating of "the vegetation of the land" (v. 2) represents the great amount of killing and destruction that the coming Assyrians would do. The pictures of locust plagues in Joel 2 and Revelation 9:1-11 both appear to represent ravaging armies that devour everything. (But some prefer to understand Revelation 9:1-11 as describing actual end-time, mutant grasshoppers; others see them as demon forces.)[4]

Note that in verse 2 Amos's reason for wanting a softer judgment upon Israel is his compassion for the weakness and frailty of his fellow Israelites. He made no argument based upon their goodness or merits. The answer to prayer was based wholly on God's grace. (Compare Rom. 5:6 regarding grace and salvation.) That God, after so many powerful and awful threatenings and denunciations against Israel, would spare her for a bit more time simply in answer to the prophet's prayer shows the desire and willingness of God to hear intercessory prayer for mercy.

B. VISION OF THE FIRE (7:4-6)

Because the Northern Kingdom would not listen to the per-

2. C. F. Keil and F. Delitzsch, *The Twelve Minor Prophets* (Grand Rapids: Eerdmans, n.d.), 1:306-7.
3. William Gesenius, *Hebrew and Chaldee Lexicon,* ed. S. P. Tregelles (Grand Rapids: Eerdmans, 1957), p. 165.
4. On locusts of Revelation 9 see chapter 12 of Gary G. Cohen, *The Horsemen Are Coming* (Chicago: Moody, 1979), for a vivid portrayal in a novel.

suasions of the Lord when He spoke to them through His prophets (2:11-12), God would "contend with them by fire" (v. 4). The word translated "contend" is *riv*, "to contend forensically, to plead a cause." So God declares in this vision that He will communicate with this willfully deaf people with "fire."[5] The commentator Maurer, based on 4:6-11, thought that this was the fire of drought. Grotius took the fire to be the invasion of the Assyrian kings. However the fire here might be just that, a heavenly fire such as that which destroyed Sodom and Gomorrah about 2,000 B.C. (Gen. 19; cf. Rev. 18:8-10). The severity of the fire is shown by the fact that it "consumed the great deep" (v. 4). *Tahom*, "the deep," is the word in Genesis 7:11 for the subterranean flood waters that were pitched upward to meet the rains falling from the sky at the time of the Flood.

The fire then "began to consume the farm land" (v. 4). Keil has suggested that the "farm land" being consumed represents the partial destruction that would come to Israel, God's own farm land (cf. Isa. 5:1-7; Mark 12:1-12), after God's judgment had fallen on the heathen world ("the great deep").[6] Such a thorough judgment is represented that it is as if both the unseen roots and the visible surface area are destroyed without a trace. Amos could not bear this, and again he prayed to God for mercy, and the vision of fire was halted. God granted Amos's plea for mercy because when the Assyrians finally took Samaria and the Northern Kingdom, they did not destroy Israel, but rather were content to scatter the Israelites and mix them into the nations.

C. VISION OF THE PLUMB LINE (7:7-9)

A plumb line is a weight hung from a string in order to measure a perfectly straight vertical line in engineering and construction work. Such a device was known in antiquity. The modern English word is derived from the Latin *plumbum*, "lead," for the heavy lead weight hung at the bottom of the string. Here the words, "Behold I am about to put a plumb line in the midst of My people Israel. I will spare them no longer" (v. 8), reveal the meaning of the vision. God is seen making

5. Gesenius, p. 767.
6. Keil and Delitzsch, 1:308-9.

careful and precise preparations for the coming punishment of the Northern Kingdom. As a surveyor He is measuring exactly where the punishment will come, how far it will extend, and the precise level of damage that it will do.

God also might be measuring time and marking the year 721 B.C. as the decreed moment for His longsuffering to end and His destruction to take place. The exasperated expression, "no longer," signifies the extent of the Lord's patience—He had spared the Northern Kingdom for 170 years, from Jeroboam I to Jeroboam II (931-761 B.C.), even though the golden calf was worshiped at the altar of Bethel. We thus learn that the raging of armies is within God's providential control, and that the armies often carry out His judgment (Isa. 10:5-6).

America's position as a bastion of religious freedom and a nation used of God for two centuries to stand for Him and to send missionaries around the globe well befits America's comparison to the words "My people" (v. 8). In her 210th year as the Northern Kingdom, Israel was destroyed for her sins by a rising, wicked nation. Amid a rising of world Communism, Israel's example stands as a harsh but clear warning to America.

In verse 9 God announces the final, utter removal of Samaria's false religious system, namely "the high places" where Baal was worshiped in the forests. The name "Isaac" here is merely another name for Israel. "The sanctuaries" (*miqdashim*, "holy places"—used of the Tabernacle, Exod. 25:8) of Bethel and Dan would be pulled down. "The house of Jeroboam" probably refers to Jeroboam I, who, as its first king, was the "father" of the Northern Kingdom. The overthrow of the false religion was certainly coming because He who rules all nations had already measured it out with His sovereign plumb line. It is interesting that Amos did not pray to stop the judgment of this third vision.

D. HISTORICAL INTERLUDE: OPPOSITION AT BETHEL (7:10-17)

1. *Amaziah's report* (7:10-11)

Amaziah, the priest of Bethel, resorted to a typical ploy of the unrighteous when he attempted to get God's spokesman condemned by the authorities. Amaziah's report against Amos attempted to enlist the king's support by showing that Amos was really just a foe of the king. It is not clear if it was Amaziah himself who was primarily vexed by Amos's denouncing of the golden calf altar around which the mixed worship pivoted. (See Luke 23:1-2 where the high priests, in a similar fashion, sought to have Pilate do away with Jesus.)

Amos did not "conspire against" the king, as Amaziah charged. The prophet who condemns the evil is not the cause of the evil, or of the punishment that follows the evil. Similarly, in 1 Kings 18:17, wicked Ahab accused Elijah by his question of denunciation, "Is this you, you troubler of Israel?" Note Elijah's classic reply, "I have not troubled Israel, but you and your father's house have, because you have forsaken the commandments of the LORD, and you have followed the Baals" (v. 18).

In modern days, however, we must not confuse a righteous-sounding church troublemaker, one who would disrupt the peace over some unimportant technicality (the spirit of phariseeism), with the prophets of old who denounced obvious, gross sins.

"The land is unable to endure all his words" (v. 10). The word *endure* in the Hebrew is *kul,* "to hold, contain—properly used of a vessel, 1 Kg 8:27."[7] An English play on the sound of this Hebrew verb would be, "The land is not able *to stay cool* at all his words." The bite of Amos's condemnation of the sins of Israel's people was in *the truth* of his words. They hated him for such rebuke, just as in another day they hated the Lord Himself for the same reason (e.g., Matt. 23:32-35). Read Matthew 10:22-25 and consider how it will be for servants of God in every generation when the Amaziahs rise up against them.

Perhaps Amaziah had heard the words of verse 9 that "the house of Jeroboam" would be smitten with "the sword," and perhaps he had chosen to interpret that to be a treasonous remark that predicted and invited the death of Jeroboam II. In any case, Jeroboam II died a natural death (2 Kings 14:29), but his house fell by "the sword" when his son Zechariah was assassinated and replaced by another family (2 Kings 15:10).

Amos certainly prophesied of the exile of Israel, as Amaziah further charged. But nothing is recorded of any action taken against the prophet because of Amaziah's words. It may be that, because of Israel's strong military position at the time,

7. Gesenius, p. 386.

Jeroboam II had a good laugh at the crazy prophet of doom whose circuit apparently had now taken him to Bethel (v. 13). King Jeroboam may even have preferred Amos to be at Bethel, for as long as Amos was there he was not in Samaria to pester the king directly.

2. *Amaziah's rebuke* (7:12-13)

Amaziah in Hebrew is *Amaz-iah* (pronounced *Ometz-Yah,* "strong [is] Yahweh"). Here the priest with so holy a name rebuked God's true servant. Amaziah addressed Amos by the title *chozeh,* "seer," because prophets often saw visions, and Amos recently might have stingingly related those visions of chapter 7 within range of Amaziah's hearing. The priest of the golden calf altar "showed Amos the end of Israel" in the sense that he told him to leave Bethel and return south to his own country of Judah, where the prophet was told to earn his living ("there eat bread") and to do his preaching.

"But no longer prophesy at Bethel" (v. 13). For two reasons the priest urged Amos not to prophesy in Bethel. Those two arguments were that that city was "a sanctuary of the king" (literally, "a holy-place royal"), that is, no less than the kings of Israel had established the city with its calf altar; and it was "a royal residence" (literally, "a house of royalty"), signifying that the king himself visited or even lived there from time to time. It would be too embarrassing to have Amos stay in town and stir up a protest march when the king came on a visit. Thus, in his first argument, Amaziah looks to human authoritarian approval to counter the force of the prophet's rebuke. In his second argument, Amaziah shows that he never really searched his own heart concerning the validity of Amos's words. Instead, he was only concerned with getting the prophet out of town before the king might visit, because Amaziah seemed to think the king was too important to be disturbed by that pest Amos. In certain situations these might be fine sentiments, but in this case, the king was leading the nation in continual sin against God. Unless he was confronted with what he was doing, the entire nation would soon be destroyed. Amaziah would have done better had he arranged for Amos to have an audience with the king.

3. *Amos's reply* (7:14-15)

By declaring, "I am not a prophet. . . . But . . . the LORD said to me, 'Go prophesy to My people Israel,'" Amos showed that he clearly understood the thoughts of Amaziah. Amaziah had told him to get out of town and make his living as a seer elsewhere. Amos answered decisively that Amaziah had missed the point. Amos was not a traveling minstrel working the area for cash. His words "I am not a prophet . . . I am a herdsman" attempted to show Amaziah that he was not a *professional* religionist who wanted to rival Amaziah for the largest following. Rather, God Himself called Amos to give a message of rebuke and judgment to the wayward people of the Northern Kingdom. Note how poignantly the imperative of verse 12 is contrasted with that of verse 15. In verse 12 Amaziah orders Amos, "*Go flee you to the land of Judah*"; but in verse 15 Amos replies that God had earlier ordered him, "*Go prophesy unto My people Israel.*" Here I have given the Hebrew word order, which makes it easier to see the "Go flee"–"Go prophesy" contrast. The contrast shows that man's wishes and God's commands are often at extreme opposition to one another.

4. *Amaziah's reward* (7:16-17)

To that one who wanted Amos's message of judgment against the Northern Kingdom stopped, God addresses a castigation of the utmost severity: "Your wife will become a harlot in the city" (v. 17). The word spoken of Amaziah's wife is *zanah*, "to commit fornication." Thus Amos's stinging rebuke to the clergyman who seeks to silence Amos's denunciation of the immorality of the day was, "Your wife [Amaziah's]" would end up in such desperate conditions that for survival she would turn to the most demeaning, illegal, and immoral form of self-support. In his sophistication, Amaziah resented Amos's direct, upbraiding speech, which indicated there would be a disruption of the smooth, royal high society in which he and his wife mingled. The cities of Samaria and Bethel, with their false religion, pseudo-sophistication, and immorality, would be destroyed and degraded by the ungodly Assyrians. Those who longed to engage in so much paganism would soon feel what the forces of complete paganism would bring when unleashed upon a group.

Women, whose husbands had been slain, would turn to prostitution to earn a living. Men and women, who were the children of Amos's day, would be slain by the Assyrian sword. The land of Israel would be divided by the conquerors and given away to foreign people. The nation of Israel would "certainly go from its land into exile" (v. 17).

14

SIN BRINGS SACKCLOTH

E. VISION OF THE SUMMER FRUIT (8:1-14)

1. *The sinful condition of Israel* (8:1-6)

a. Ripe fruit (8:1-3). Amos is now shown his fourth vision, "a basket of summer fruit." Just as we in America have a double year of sorts with the calendar year of January to December and the school year of September to June, so ancient Israel had a double year system. The *religious year* went from Nisan (also called Aviv) to Adar, our March to February (Exod. 12:2), while the *agricultural year* went from Tishri to Elul, September to late August. This is why Jewish people observe *Rosh Hashanah* ("beginning-of-the-year") in September.

Therefore, "summer fruit" is an expression with a double play on words. First, the Hebrew word *ka-yi-tz* means "summer fruit," that is, "end-of-the-year fruit." Such fruit was usually figs (cf. Jer. 24; 40:10, 12). Second, the word sounds similar to *qetz*, which means "the end."[1] Thus in this fourth vision God showed Amos a vision of a basket of fruit and then pronounced, "The end [*qetz*] has come for My people Israel." The finality of the imagery was terrifying. As those figs had finally reached their year-end time of plucking, so Israel had at last arrived at her end. God would not allow her to live any longer upon the tree of nations; He was about to yank her down and cast her into the basket for Assyria to devour.

"I will spare them no longer" (v. 2). Examining the Hebrew in this expression is like taking a telescope and looking at a remarkable double star. That is so because it contains two very interesting and similar plays on words. One pivots on the word translated "Joseph" and the other on the word translated "He-

1. William Gesenius, *Hebrew and Chaldee Lexicon,* ed. S. P. Tregelles (Grand Rapids: Eerdmans, 1957), pp. 731, 737.

brew," although from the English this is impossible to see. Literally this clause reads, "Not I-shall-add longer sparing him."

The first play on words is based upon "not I shall add," which is taken from the same root (*yasaf*) as the name "Joseph." The basic meaning is "to add" or "to increase" (Gen. 30:24).[2] Here God says to the Northern Kingdom, which was known as "the house of Joseph" (5:6), "I will Joseph *spare* [that is, "add to you"] you no longer." Joseph was perhaps the greatest recipient of God's blessing and of God's preservation in the patriarchal period. Now God announces that he will no longer "Joseph" them; His blessing and preservation would no more be upon them.

The second item pivots on the other word translated "spare," *'eber*, "to cross over, to pass over (usually a river)." From this same root comes the word *Hebrew*, "those who have come from afar and who have *passed over* into the land."[3] (The word *passover*, which refers to the exodus from Egypt, is *pasach*, an entirely different word.) Therefore, in what appears to be another play on words, God announced that He would no longer "Hebrew" the Northern Kingdom. The Hebrew reader thus hears God's frightful announcement, "I will no longer Joseph or Hebrew them." Thus, just as summer fruit that is ripe for being devoured or allowed to rot, so God's distinctive blessings would be removed from them.

"The songs ... wailing .... silence" (v. 3). The wicked can sing their songs of scorn in God's face for only so long. Finally, when the period of God's endurance is fulfilled, He permits the wicked to consume one another, and the ballads of sinful pleasures turn into "wailing" and finally into the "silence" of resignation. (See Psalm 95:8-11; Heb. 2:3; 3:12; 2 Pet. 3:9.) The imagery is strong and stark. Those who sing their blasphemous songs amid the riotous and wanton living of Jeroboam II's palaces would soon have no song to sing amid the death that the Assyrians would cause. The child of God, however, will someday have "a new song" that will triumph over death (Rev. 14:3).

b. Ripe nation (8:4-6). The previous three verses showed that the Northern Kingdom was reaching the point at which it

2. Ibid., p. 354.
3. Ibid., pp. 601-4.

would be fully ripe for judgment. Now, in the next three verses
the sins of moral decay in Israel are described.

Israel was conducting harmful and dishonest business practices. She trampled the needy. Here the word *sha'af* means "to
pant after, to breathe hard in racing after the prey." God saw
Israel racing at full speed to catch up with the needy so she
could pounce upon them as a wolf pounces upon a lamb. (See
Isa. 59:7.) She was doing away with the humble, literally
"causing them to cease" (from the Hebrew word *sabbath*, or
shabat as the modern Israelis pronounce it).

The wicked leaders in Israel were eager for God's holy days
to be over so they could get back to their cheating of the poor.
Verses 4 and 5 contain an ironic play on words based on the
word *sabbath*, which is used twice. In verse 4 the wicked
caused the humble (poor) to cease—"to be sabbathed"—while in
verse 5 the wicked could hardly endure the Sabbath day, so
anxious were they to return to their robberies. The strength
of Amos's imagery again rises to its heights here. He is not
portraying people who merely break the Sabbath, but rather
those who loathe the Sabbath—loathe it perhaps partly because
they do not want their souls and spirits turned to God, which
would make them feel guilty over their sins.

In contrast to the above-described anti-Sabbath attitude, it
should be noted that for centuries many Jewish people, including today's modern Israelis have had a partylike celebration on
Friday evenings called *oneg shabbat*, "delightful sabbath." The
life of Christ showed that the Sabbath was to be a time of rest,
worship, showing God's mercy, and performing necessities. The
Pharisees unfortunately went to another extreme and made it
an unhappy day of catching people in violations of their own
man-made ordinances.

In their abuse of the poor, the people of Samaria had become
so hardened and bereft of mercy that they allowed persons to
be sold into slavery in order to secure from them such items as a
pair of shoes (v. 6). Why did the wicked do that? Verse 6
answers, "For money." (See also Mic. 3:11; Matt. 21:12-13;
1 Tim. 6:10.)

Finally, they sold "refuse" as if it were the genuine commod-
ity (v. 6). Such dealing typifies all of Satan's counterfeit dealing in this world. From the very beginning he has sold false-

hood to the simple as truth, happiness, and righteousness—for the price of their souls. Eventually his evil merchandise always turns out to be refuse. (See Gen. 3:4-7; 2 Cor. 11:14; Rev. 18: 10-11.)

2. *The suffering coming to Israel* (8:7-14)

a. Sackcloth for dress (8:7-10). This section begins with a divine oath sworn "by the pride of Jacob" (v. 7). Keil and Maurer take "the pride of Jacob" to be God Himself, as "the pride of Israel" is in Hosea 5:5 and 7:10; Calvin sees it as "the privileges of Israel"; Jamieson suggests that it refers to "the Temple." But it could refer to the arrogance of the Northern Kingdom. The word *gaon* ("pride") can connote either "glory, splendor," as in Isaiah 4:2 and 60:15, or "pride, arrogance," as in Proverbs 16:18. God's oath that He will never forget Israel's evil deeds need not disturb us, because it was made to an absolutely unrepentant nation. This doctrine conforms with all of Scripture, including the New Testament. The Lord does not forget or pass over the sins of the unrepentant. Contrast this with Psalm 103:12 and 1 John 1:9.

"Will not the land quake and everyone . . . mourn?" (v. 8). It is difficult to be certain whether here in 8:8 we have words predicted before or after the great quake mentioned in 1:1—words explaining that the quake was or would be God's judgment. In either case the prophet at least has shown that a natural disaster could be the result of God's disapproval of a nation. The Flood of Genesis 6-8 was certainly the height of such happenings, as was the destruction of Sodom and Gomorrah (Gen. 19:24). In those two Genesis events, however, the disasters were pronounced as direct supernatural interventions, whereas in Amos we are not told specifically how the event would occur. Rather, we are told that such a calamity was inevitable in the case of so sinful a nation. Amos, however, was a prophet who received special revelation from God. On the other hand, when we see individual natural disasters, we should be most hesitant to declare them as God's judgments.

"It will rise up like the Nile" (v. 8). God now vows that the judgment He will send upon the Northern Kingdom will: shake the land, rise like the Nile, toss about, and subside like the Nile.

The Nile River flows north from the Sudan, where the White and Blue Niles meet at Khartoum. In June the water turns green from the microorganisms; in July the color becomes red as the organisms die. Then from August through October the waters rise twenty-one to twenty-five feet in good years. If the river rises less than twenty-one feet, the lateral water flooding is insufficient. If it rises more than twenty-eight feet, the towns along it become flooded. This "life of Egypt" river, "El Nil," leaves not only its irrigating waters but also a thin red-brown layer of natural fertilizer that annually renews the land.

By using earthquake and river metaphors God has pictured the initial, violent *shaking* of the Assyrian attack, which would be followed by the *rising floods* of invading Assyrians. The *tossing* of the waters pictures the havoc that would be raised by the Assyrians once they had conquered Samaria and had begun to deport the population and replace it with foreigners. Finally, after thoroughly subjugating the land, the Assyrians would *subside* like the Nile and would withdraw the major portion of their armies back into Assyria.

"I shall make the sun go down at noon" (v. 9). Here God portrays as a premature darkening of the sky the great calamity that would befall Samaria. That nation, after Jeroboam II's recent local conquests, seemed to have risen to a new grandeur, "noon," when the sun is at its zenith. However, God will not let that light continue its normal course, but will cut it off suddenly and totally. Darkness is often used in Scripture to signify calamity and God's displeasure (cf. Jer. 15:9; Ezek. 32:7-10; Mark 15:33).

These words concerning the sun and darkening are similar to Christ's words in Matthew 24:29 concerning the end of the present age. It need not be assumed that both references speak of the same event, especially in such different contexts. It is sufficient to say that both descriptions tell about cataclysmic events that would close different eras.

"Then I shall turn your festivals into mourning" (v. 10). Because the appeals of the prophets had failed to change Samaria's calf-worshiping festivals into ones that were characterized by right worship and repentance, God declares that He will remove the offensive festivals (5:21). The word *turn* is *haphach,* "to turn as a cake" (Hos. 7:8). It is used when speaking of the overthrow of cities (4:11; Gen. 19:21, 25).[4] If the people will not turn their hearts from sin to holiness, then God will turn their outward circumstances from blessing to cursing, as He promised in Deuteronomy 27:11–28:68 and 30:19. Now they shall see mourning replacing their festivals; sackcloth instead of their splendid robes; baldness (shaved heads) instead of the lavish coiffures that once graced the heads; and a time of bitterness over being separated from their children by the cruelties of the conquerors (Zech. 12:10).

Those events are described here as a "bitter day." The word for "bitter" is *mar*, and this word is preserved in Exodus 15:23 where the bitter lake to which Israel came was named *Marah*. There the Israelites had grumbled to Moses that the water was undrinkable. Perhaps the Lord had that incident in mind when He said, "I shall turn your festivals into mourning." The result of their sins would be a bitter drink (Zech. 12:2; cf. Luke 22:42; Rev. 17:4 on cup metaphor).

b. Famine from God's Word (8:11-14). After announcing the physical suffering and violence that was soon to fall upon the Northern Kingdom, the Word of the Lord now proclaims the spiritual suffering that would befall the nation. To those who did not wish to hear God's Word, God proclaims they shall have their desire granted—He will stop speaking to them (cf. Rom. 1:24, 26, 28). A *famine* normally implies two elements: (1) a serious lack of food over a period of time, and (2) a great need and gnawing desire for that food among the population. So in these verses God's announcement looks to a future time when there would be no prophet and no teaching of God's Word in Samaria. It would be a time when the people at last would crave and hunger for the Word—but without satisfaction. This condition of spiritual famine generally lingered up to the time of Christ, by which time the religious errors of the "Samaritans" had become proverbial (John 1:46—Nazareth was in the Samaria region; John 4:9).

"And people will stagger . . . to seek the word of the Lord" (v. 12). The famine for the Word of God now causes hungry people "to stagger," *nua'*. This Hebrew word is used for drunk-

4. Ibid., p. 230.

ards and the blind (Prov. 5:6; Isa. 24:20).[5] From "sea to sea"
is an expression referring to the area between the Mediterranean Sea and the Dead Sea (or possibly the Sea of Galilee).
The survivors of God's judgment and their offspring will now
crave what their fathers had despised and refused.

After the fall of the Northern Kingdom, the prophets spoke
primarily to Judah until she too was taken captive and destroyed
in 586 B.C. Then they spoke to the exiles, and then to the Jews
who returned to Judah years later. However, as Amos prophesied, long gaps began to appear when no prophetic voice was
heard. From 690-650 B.C., after Isaiah, there was no prophetic
word; from 492-437, there was no prophetic voice. Then, from
Malachi (420 B.C.) to John the Baptist, A.D. 26 (446 years),
neither written nor spoken word came from God. And now,
from the end of the first century until the present, the scattered
children of Israel have not yet fully opened their ears to hear
the word of the greatest of all the prophets, the Son of God
Himself. Could the Lord Jesus have had this very part of Amos
in mind when He spoke the words of Matthew 5:6, "Blessed are
those who hunger and thirst for righteousness, for they shall be
satisfied"? The end of the spiritual famine and drought had
come for those who fed upon Christ, the Bread of Life and the
giver of living water (John 4:10; 6:48; 7:37-38).

"The beautiful virgins and the young men" (v. 13). The
healthiest and most robust will be among those who suffer from
this famine of God's Word (v. 11). Those who have the best
years of their lives before them will thirst for God's assurance,
encouragement, and guidance amid harsh days for their people.
The children and older people accept the status quo, but the
young adults need God's guidance so much—and there will be
little of it. Again, Matthew 5:6 is God's answer to such a situation.

"As for those who swear by the guilt of Samaria" (v. 14). The
"guilt of Samaria" is the calf altars at Dan and Bethel. Those
of Samaria swore their oaths with the formula "As your god
lives, O Dan," rather than "As Jehovah lives," or "As the LORD
lives." They were guilty of an idolatrous worship of Jehovah.
Their fate would be worse than that of the new young genera-

5. Ibid., p. 540.

tion who would thirst and faint—namely, those idolaters were earmarked for absolute judgment, to "fall and not rise again." (Compare Isaiah 40:30-31.)

Amos's mention of Beersheba, the southernmost city of ancient united Israel (and part of Judah), shows that religious pilgrimages to that city of Abraham and Isaac (Gen. 21:31; 26:33) were probably active yet in the eighth century B.C. Such pilgrimages, like all religious works that are accompanied by false ceremonies and wicked lives, are of no avail. Thus, God's prophet declares that those who rely on their oaths made upon the calf altars and who journey far, merely to return home to sin, "will fall and not rise again." Surely the message to Samaria also is clear to the modern nations that are living in excessive luxury.

15

GOD BRINGS RESTORATION

F. VISION OF THE LORD BESIDE THE ALTAR (9:1-10)

1. *The present destruction of the sinful kingdom* (9:1-6)

a. The holy pursuit (9:1-4). This section begins with Amos's fifth vision, in which he beholds *"the Lord standing beside the altar"* (v. 1). In this passage the great question that the commentators over the years have addressed is, What altar is here before us? Such ancient and modern names as Cyril, Ewald, Hitzig, Hofmann, Baur, and Jamieson believed this to be Israel's altar and temple, with golden calf, at Bethel. On the other hand, Calvin, Fairbairn, and Keil thought it to be the altar and Temple of the entire nation, in Jerusalem.[1]

Those who believe the altar to be the Bethel altar and temple see 9:1 as a continuation of chapter 8, which ended with evildoers swearing by this false shrine. The picture then is one in which God strikes the top of the temple and causes it to fall upon the wicked people below, who are idolatrously trusting in it and the golden calf astride it.

Those who think this temple to be the Jerusalem Temple believe that Amos is now speaking of both Israel and Judah, as he did in 2:4 and 2:6, in which he cited both for judgment.

Both explanations are sensible and both fit history, because Samaria and Bethel fell in 721 B.C., and Jerusalem fell in 586 B.C. Both theories also have famous and revered commentators supporting them. It would seem, however, that only persons from the Northern Kingdom would hide atop Mt. Carmel, which is located in the north country. That indication in verse 3 best settles the question concerning the altar. Starting at verse 7, we have in view the restoration of the entire nation.

1. C. F. Keil and F. Delitzsch, *The Twelve Minor Prophets* (Grand Rapids: Eerdmans, n.d.), pp. 320-23; and Robert Jamieson, A. R. Fausset, and David Brown, *Commentary on the Whole Bible* (Grand Rapids: Zondervan, 1962), pp. 800-801.

Therefore, the Lord is seen in verse 1 as smashing down the false temple of either Dan or Bethel in the Northern Kingdom. He strikes the top, "the capitals," with such force that it breaks apart even to its foundations ("thresholds"). It then falls upon the people's heads. This is figurative language to show what will befall the nation because of its idolatrous worship. Those temples, however, eventually collapsed. Many of the scattered people of Samaria were later killed as fugitives and refugees by the sword of the Assyrians and other nations that pursued them through the centuries (see Deut. 28:64-67).

"They will not have a fugitive . . . or a refugee" (v. 1). The Lord is engaged here in a holy pursuit, hunting out sinners for punishment. This verse, as explained above, describes the collapse of the idolatrous temple upon its sinful worshipers. The collapse of such a building might be viewed as destroying only the relatively few unfortunate who happened to be present at the moment of the divine earthquake. To underscore for us that the judgment and destruction is of a larger scale, the prophet adds here that no one at all will escape those punishments—no one will be a successful *fugitive* (one who *flees* the force of a calamity) or *refugee* (one who *finds refuge or safety* after a calamity).

"Though they dig into Sheol . . . ascend to heaven" (v. 2). From a human foe some, either by skill, good fortune, or bribery, may escape. However, Amos assures the arrogant ones of Samaria and Bethel that there shall be no escape from God, not even in Sheol (the unseen world of the grave and beyond). The people must repent of their sins, cast away their idolatrous worship, and come to Jehovah for mercy at the true altar of sacrifice (cf. Heb. 2:3).

Compare the words of Amos 9:2 with the similar wording of Deuteronomy 30:12, and with Paul's quotation of that Deuteronomy passage in Romans 10:6-7. Both Moses and Paul adjure all people that no one need dig down into Sheol or ascend into heaven to please God or to find His salvation. It is near, available through obedience and faith.

"And though they hide on the summit of Carmel" (v. 3). One not familiar with the land might think that a hiding place on the summit of a mountain would be easily discovered. Modern people, accustomed to seeing the tops of mountains laid bare by the lenses of aerial cameras, are especially prone to such thinking. Mount Carmel has about sixty square miles of area at the summit, with about thirty square miles available for hiding. One could easily hide amid the many trees, caves, rocks, and crevasses. However, Amos says God will lead the foreign pursuers to such a fugitive. Even if one were to submerge to "the floor of the sea," God would send a serpent to bite such a refugee. The top of Carmel and the floor of the sea are part of the Hebrew parallelism and correspond to heaven and Sheol in verse 2.

"And though they go into captivity" (v. 4). In the book of Genesis, Joseph was taken captive into Egypt. Here at last, as Potiphar's slave, he was safe from his brothers' hatred, he had a good job, and he was well off in every way (Gen. 39:1-6). In contrast to this, Amos paints the awful picture of a captivity that would not equal safety or happiness for those who survived the destruction of the Northern Kingdom. In the centuries to come the descendants of those survivors continually would be subject to murders and slaughters in all the countries where the Lord would cause them to be driven.

"And I will set My eyes against them for evil and not for good" (v. 4). This is the fulfillment and confirmation of God's words spoken by Moses in Deuteronomy 28:63. Because of their continual practice of sin and their accompanying hardness of heart that, in effect, caused them to shout the prophets into silence (2:11-12), the chosen people were now chosen for God's cursing instead of His blessing. There is quite a lesson here for every nation or person who reads these words and the words of Deuteronomy 27:11—28:68.

b. The holy Person (9:5-6). After the pronouncement of doom upon the Northern Kingdom, which denunciation actually went as far back as 2:6, Amos here gives a fitting affirmation that Jehovah is the true, living, and powerful God who sustains this world. Verse 5 begins with His title of military might, "The Lord GOD [Jehovah] of hosts" (Hebrew, *Adonai Yahweh Tzivaoth*), and verse 6 concludes, "The LORD [Jehovah] is His name." Both occasions use the identical four letter sacred spelling, *YHWH* (i.e., *Yahweh*, Jehovah), despite the lower case/upper case difference from verse 5 to verse 6, in the English rendering of the name.

Jehovah, not any other, is the one who causes the *rising and falling of the Nile* of Egypt (v. 5). The excavations of Samaria, in 1931 and subsequently, have discovered images of the Egyptian gods Isis and Horus, *the wife and son of Osiris the Nile god.* Thus, by comparing Jehovah's control of the world to the rising and subsiding of the Nile,[2] Amos here in verse 5 may be replying to those in the Northern Kingdom who honored the Nile gods, whether openly or secretly.

"His vaulted dome" (v. 6). Here the *New American Standard Bible* (NASB) translation says that God "has founded His *vaulted dome* over the earth," but the King James Version reads, "Founded his *troop* in the earth" (italics added in both verses). The Hebrew word is *agudah,* from the root *agud,* "to bind, to tie together in a bundle." Therefore *agudah* has such meanings as: a knot; a bundle, as of hyssop (Exod. 12:22); a troop of men, bundled or knotted together (2 Sam. 2:25); the arch of heaven, knotted together.[3] From this list of meanings it should be clear that it would be totally improper for anyone to think, on the basis of one elaborate English translation of *agudah,* that Amos is supporting any medieval theory that the sky is some sort of solid copper dome. Unfortunately, the very expression "vaulted dome" brings to mind for many persons a picture of a gothic vaulted ceiling—totally foreign to Amos's day. Rather, Amos affirms that God has created "His bundle" over the earth. This "bundle" may be viewed as one containing stars, air, clouds, or all three. It is a bundle that has been *knotted together* by the hand of the Creator. The one who does all this is not the calf of Bethel, before whom Jeroboam II bowed and sacrificed when he visited the royal altar on one of his junkets. On the contrary, "*Jehovah is His name!*"

2. *The future restoration of the righteous kingdom* (9:7-15)

a. The sinful in Israel removed (9:7-8*a*). To set the background for His grand announcement of future reclamation, God first took away Israel's reliance upon her position of special privilege, based on her lineage from Abraham, Isaac, and Jacob.

2. Joseph P. Free, *Archeology and Bible History* (Wheaton, Ill.: Scripture Press, 1956), pp. 193-94.
3. William Gesenius, *Hebrew and Chaldee Lexicon,* ed. S. P. Tregelles (Grand Rapids: Eerdmans, 1957), p. 10.

Now, in God's eyes, she had made herself the same as the Ethiopians. Also her privileged status, based on God's deliverance of her from Egypt, was to be regarded no more specially than God's moving the Philistines or the Syrians from their respective places of origin.

How could God reduce Israel this way in light of Exodus 12:23 and 20:2, wherein He claims a special ownership over her because He spared her firstborn children on the basis of the shed blood and delivered the nation from Egyptian slavery? The answer is that Israel repeatedly broke His covenant, and by her continued gross sinfulness suspended that bond of special ownership and privilege between herself and Jehovah. Therefore this "sinful kingdom . . . I will destroy it from the face of the earth." Truly, after the Assyrian invasion, the Northern Kingdom was forever gone, never again to be restored as a separate entity.

b. The remnant out of Israel retained (9:8b-10). Amid this storm of judgment pronounced by the Lord through his servant Amos, a faint bell of hope is suddenly heard, as if from a lighthouse amid the roaring waves: "Nevertheless, I will not totally destroy the house of Jacob" (v. 8b). The Lord thereby qualifies the declaration made earlier in this verse, "I will destroy. . . ." In His limitation God uses the identical Hebrew word *shamad*, "to destroy, lay waste," as He did in the first part of the verse. The qualification also uses the characteristic Hebrew doubling to show great emphasis and intensity. It reads literally, "Nevertheless, destroying I will not destroy," and it clearly pledges a prohibition on the total destruction of Jacob's house. The title "house of Jacob" includes the people of both the Northern and Southern Kingdoms. This title shows that in some way the holy God still was mindful of His promises to Abraham, Isaac, and Jacob, and would therefore save His people's existence through preserving a remnant. So the apostle Paul in Romans 11:28 could look back and say of Israel, "They are beloved for the sake of the fathers" (i.e., for the sake of God's fulfilling His promises to the patriarchs someday to give them the land of Israel forever in a condition of righteousness and peace. See Jeremiah 30:11; Romans 11:11-36).

"And I will shake the house of Jacob among all nations . . .

but not a kernel will fall to the ground" (v. 9). A sieve is a device used for the separation and aeration of grain. It mechanically removes bad or swollen kernels, as well as other pieces of impurity, and it aerates and fluffs out that which passes through. Thus both the purity and the consistency of the sifted grain are improved. By that picture God helps us harmonize His statements that He would destroy the Northern Kingdom forever and yet preserve the house of Jacob. The Assyrian invasion of Samaria and the subsequent Babylonian invasion of Judah would serve to destroy the unrighteous kingdoms. However, through all those invasions and scatterings of Israel, God would preserve His elect remnant so perfectly that not even one repentant person would perish. (See Deut. 30:1-4.) This perfect preservation of the remnant of Israel explains why in the end time God can seal on their foreheads twelve thousand of each of the twelve tribes (Rev. 7:3-8). Today we may not be able to sort out accurately the house of Jacob into its tribal lineage, but He who will not let even so much as one kernel fall inadvertantly can sort out those sifted, separated, and finally purified ones.

Verse 10, however, reminds us afresh that the sinners of Israel, although they may still call themselves *My people*, will die by the sword." Note the two extremes in verses 9 and 10. The wicked sinners *will all perish* despite their claims of blood relationship to Jacob and their claims still to be God's special people. On the other hand, the remnant by God's grace *will all survive*, and not even one of them (not one "kernel") will fall to the ground.[4]

c. The house of David repaired (9:11-12). "In that day I will raise up the fallen booth of David" (v. 11). The Hebrew word for *booth* is *sukkah*, of which the plural *sukkoth* is used in the title Feast of Booths or Tabernacles (Lev. 23:34; Deut. 16: 13). A booth was a temporary dwelling, usually made of branches, sticks, and leaves. (This is not to be confused with a tent, or the grand tentlike Tabernacle in the wilderness, which

4. Compare Revelation 7:1-8 with Revelation 14:1-3. Notice that despite the persecutions by Antichrist in Revelation 11-13 not one of the 144,000 sealed in chapter 7 fails to make it to the heavenly or Millennial Mount Zion in chapter fourteen. Every "kernel" of the 144,000, despite the sifting, arrives safely in the end. See also Gary G. Cohen, *Understanding Revelation* (Chicago: Moody, 1978).

would be made of skins or other durable cloth.) Here in this verse the word is used "contemptuously of a small ruined house," according to Gesenius. But Tregelles disagrees and says of Gesenius's comment, "It is difficult to see what idea of contempt is contained in the passage."[5] Perhaps God calls it a booth out of pity, because the Israel that David had ruled and subdued was now a divided kingdom. "In that day" refers to God's end-time restoration of Israel, which restoration was never fulfilled in the regatherings under Zerubbabel (536 B.C.), Ezra (458 B.C.), or Nehemiah (445 B.C.), or anytime thereafter.

God promises prophetically that He will: (1) raise up David's fallen house, that He will restore the land to Israel and the rule to the Davidic family; (2) "wall up its breaches," cause the holes and gaps in the walls surrounding the city of Jerusalem to be filled;[6] (3) "raise up its ruins," that is, God will restore that which is left of the people of Israel and of the promised land, both physically and spiritually (Isa. 65:17-25; Jer. 31:31-40; Ezek. 37:1-14; Zech. 12-14);[7] and (4) "rebuild it as in the days of old," that is, God will yet restore the nation to its grandeur and glory as in the days of David and Solomon, when it was the glory of nations and when royalty from afar came to visit its gates and Temple (2 Sam. 7:10-16; Zech. 14:16-21).

The boundaries of the future restored Israel will extend to the borders that she held under Solomon. This will include Edom, which is located south of Judah and the Dead Sea, and which traditionally has been at enmity with both houses of Israel. The boundaries will include other surrounding lands, which in the end-time restoration also will be "called by My

5. Gesenius, p. 585, with Tregelles's editorial comments contained in brackets.
6. I recall in January 1968, a few months after the June 1967 Six-Day War, standing and staring at a breach in the wall that surrounded Jerusalem on the east side, by the Kidron Valley. It gave one the feeling of intense incompleteness, almost as if the rest of the walls were useless as long as that breach existed. (Cf. Psalm 106:23; Isa. 58:12; Lam. 2:13.)
7. It is my opinion that the Scripture passages cited here prove clearly and conclusively that God is not done with national Israel, and that the people will yet be regathered, converted to Christ, and restored upon their promised land forever. Amillennialism, which seeks to do away with all this by "spiritualizing," must fight against the clear statements of Jehovah concerning Israel's restoration.

name." Because the surrounding lands have belonged to pagan deities or to Islam ever since Amos spoke, the prophecy has not yet found its fulfillment. It awaits the Millennial restoration spoken of in Isaiah 11:4*b*-13; Zechariah 14:16-21; and in Revelation 20:1-6.

"Declares the Lord who does this" (v. 12). These are immense prophecies that transcend history. Except it had been the Lord Himself who uttered the words through the prophet, everyone would scoff at any hope of their fulfillment. Therefore, it is significant that the Lord Himself affirmed that He will bring all this to pass.

d. The people and land of Israel restored (9:13-15). *"The plowman will overtake the reaper . . ."* (v. 13). The idea here is that the land will yield such abundant crops that the farmers will hardly be able to keep up with the prolific bounty. As soon as one crop is cut down, a new one will be planted, and sometimes the one racing to plow will catch up with and pass the one cutting down the last crop. This circumstance will be the exact opposite of that described in 4:6-8, which speaks of God's sending a punishing drought upon the land in order to force the inhabitants to turn back to Him. The text here implies that Israel will be spiritually reborn, which will result in God's changing the drought and famine to abundant rains and luxuriant harvests.

"And the treader of grapes him who sows seed" (v. 13). Grapes are trod down in the winepress in order to yield their juice. Here the portrait is that the growth is so rapid that almost as soon as a person sows the seed, the vine has grown and the grapes have ripened. In this way the one process seems to follow the other almost instantaneously (cf. Lev. 26:5).[8] This is the kind of change that will befall the nation when it passes from God's curse to God's blessing on the occasion of its

---

8. I once planted a tiny grapevine eight inches tall. After three years it was still less than two feet high and had yielded less than a dozen grapes. In the fourth year it was moved to another side of the house and probationed for destruction, when something happened—it grew high and spread about twelve feet in that season alone, yielding countless bunches of grapes. By the fifth year it was twenty feet across, and it yielded buckets and buckets of grapes. So it will be with Israel.

getting right with God in the last days (Rom. 11:26-27). "And each of them will sit under his vine . . . with no one to make them afraid, for the mouth of the LORD of hosts has spoken" (Mic. 4:4).

See the entire fourth chapter of Micah for a full description of this future Millennial age when Israel shall be fully restored both spiritually and physically upon her land, and when at last she will acknowledge Christ as her Lord and Messiah. Zechariah 12:10; 13:1; and 14:4 are three of the great Old Testament verses that clearly and *inescapably* teach God's end-time conversion and restoration of His ancient people Israel. Ezekiel 37:15-28 further teaches that the restored nation shall be one, no longer divided into an Israel and Judah. Thus the truths of Amos are preserved, the Northern Kingdom shall never rise again as a separate nation, but Jacob shall be preserved and restored (9:8 ff.).

"Mountains will drip sweet wine, and all the hills will be dissolved" (v. 13). This is an allusion to Joel 3:18, uttered sixty years prior to Amos. The vines are seen upon the hills of Israel. (The Hebrew *har*, "mountain," should not be thought of in terms of the steep slopes of northwestern North America.) The vines are prophetically seen as being so heavy with the juice of their grapes that those grapes will be dripping even without being pressed. The Hebrew verb *moog* means "to flow, to flow down," and hence the primary meanings, derived with the aid of interpretation, become "to melt, to melt down, to be dissolved."[9] The basic translation, then, is "the hills will flow-down," which follows Joel 3:18's "the hills will flow with milk." The *New American Standard* translators have selected their translation because the form of the verb here is a reflexive, which has an intensive action. The translators figuratively interpreted the thought to be one in which the hills would flow so freely that they would "be dissolved" by their own copious liquid. It would probably be safer to see the translation of this verse patterned after Joel, "the hills will flow abundantly." The word *abundantly* is used to signify the intensity of the verb form here. All such grammatical fine points aside, the clear

9. Gesenius, p. 455.

testimony of God's Word here is that the restored Israel will experience an agricultural boom of such abundance that the cause will only be attributable to the special blessings of the true and living God.

"And I will restore the captivity of My people Israel" (v. 14). The Hebrew idiom conveys the opposite meaning of that which the English seems to convey. The English expression "restore the captivity" could mean to return a free nation back into servitude. This expression in Hebrew, however, means to restore a previously enslaved individual or group to freedom. Thus God announces that in the end time the children of Israel, once scattered by Him into Assyrian or Babylonian slavery, will be freed and will return to the promised land. This always has been the dream of the Jewish people, and one of the medals of the modern state of Israel has a motto that reads, "We shall remain free men." (See Deut. 30:1-5.)

"And they will rebuild the ruined cities and live in them" (v. 14). Recall that in 722-721 B.C. the Northern Kingdom people were driven out of their cities by the Assyrians. In 606-586 B.C. the Babylonians drove the people of Judah out of their cities. In 168 B.C. the Jews were again suffering as the Syrians drove them out of their cities; in A.D. 66-72 the Romans drove them out; in A.D. 134 the Romans under Hadrian again drove them out; in the eighth century the Muslims conquered them; in the eleventh century it was the Turks; in the twelfth and thirteenth centuries it was the European Crusaders; also in the thirteenth century there were the papal persecutions.

In the fourteenth century the Jews were expelled from Paris by Philip the Fair (1306) and from Germany when they were blamed for the "Black Death" plague (1398). In the fifteenth century they were expelled from Spain by Ferdinand and Isabella (1492—the same year in which God opened the New World wherein they could flee to safety), and from Portugal (1498). In the sixteenth century the Jews were ordered by Russia's Ivan the Terrible to be "baptized or drowned" (1563).

In more resent times the Jews continued to be persecuted. In the nineteenth century they were driven out of Romania (1866, 1870, 1873). At the start of this century they were persecuted in Austria and Germany (1900). Mobs attempted to slaughter all of the Jews in Hebron (1929). Hitler drove the Jews out of the European cities and murdered six million of them in a satanic attempt at genocide (1939-45). Under the British mandate (1917-1948) European Jews who survived the holocaust of Hitler were severely limited concerning entry into Palestine. Even today many would again cast the Jews out of their newly rebuilt cities.

Only in light of the above-listed chronicle of suffering and exile can one even come close to comprehending the grandeur and the hope that the precious promises of God found here in Amos offer to Israel.

"They will also plant vineyards and drink their wine" (v. 14). Compare Deuteronomy 28:30-53, which tells of God's curses upon the vineyards and gardens of a disobedient people, with this verse, which promises God's eventual and final end-time blessing upon the Israelites and their vineyards.

"I will also plant them on their land, and they will not again be rooted out from their land which I have given them, says the Lord your God" (v. 15). What a beautiful and wonderful ending of hope to such a strong book of judgment. By strong armies and confidence Jeroboam II could not keep the people of Israel on the land when, because of their sin, it was against God's will. But when it shall be God's will to return, cleanse, and plant the Jews upon their land, then all the nations and all the armies following Antichrist will not be able to remove them (Zech. 12:3; Rev. 3:7b; 16:16). Let every reader also settle in his mind once and for all that this verse, Amos 9:15, has never yet found its historical fulfillment—it awaits the future. Only in 1948, when the state of Israel was reestablished, has this promise even begun to be fulfilled.

The reasons for the Israelite people's final implantation and security on "their land" lies in the twin facts enunciated here in this delightful final verse of the book. *First, "I have given them"*—God is the owner of this planet by virtue of His creatorship and His being the sustainer of it by the Word of His power. All United Nations' decisions, newspaper editorials, and Palestinian claims to the contrary, the owner of the planet has the ultimate right of land disposal, because it is all His land. He, in the end, will give the ancient soil back to the children of Abraham, gathered together out of all the tribes. All of us who love Him must love His holy and wise will. We must rejoice that the land of Palestine will eventually belong forever to the Jews, and a wise foreign policy will take into account the ultimate will of the Creator when it makes its decisions. *Second,* the expression "says the Lord [Jehovah] your God" closes the book with an affirmation that a final conversion of Israel will indeed take place. Therefore the land will be prepared in which a holy God may shower His blessings upon a once belligerent people (Zech. 12:10; 13:1; 14:3-4, 16-21).[10]

Let this ending scorch its strong lesson upon the heart of every reader, to make sure he has come to the foot of the cross and by faith has embraced Christ's forgiveness. Let every reader be sure that he is standing secure upon the ground of God's blessing, rather than upon the land of sin and rebellion, wherein only sorrow and grief abide. As in the case of Israel, there is fullness of blessing only when Jehovah is in truth *your God.*

BIBLIOGRAPHY

Clow, W. *Bible Reader's Encyclopedia and Concordance.* Rev. ed. New York: Collins, 1977.

Free, Joseph P. *Archeology and Bible History.* Wheaton, Ill.: Scripture Press, 1956.

Gesenius, William. *Hebrew and Chaldee Lexicon.* Edited by S. P. Tregelles. Grand Rapids: Eerdmans, 1957.

Jamieson, Robert; Fausset, A. R.; and Brown, David. *Commentary on the Whole Bible.* Grand Rapids: Zondervan, 1962.

Josephus. *Wars of the Jews.* Philadelphia: Winston Co., 1957 ed.

Keil, C. F., and Delitzsch, F. *The Twelve Minor Prophets.* Vol. 1. Grand Rapids: Eerdmans, n.d.

Pritchard, J. B., ed. *The Ancient Near East.* Princeton, N.J.: U. Press, 1958.

Ryrie, Charles C. *The Ryrie Study Bible.* Chicago: Moody, 1978.

Thompson, William M. *The Land and the Book.* 3 vols. New York: Harper & Bros., 1880.

Walton, John H. *Chronological Charts of the Old Testament.* Grand Rapids: Zondervan, 1978.

Whitcomb, John C., Jr. *Chart of the Old Testament Kings and Prophets.* Chicago: Moody, 1968.

10. Read Gary G. Cohen, *The Horsemen Are Coming* (Chicago: Moody, 1979) for a scenario of how these final events of the age might occur.